The New Americans
Recent Immigration and American Society

Edited by
Steven J. Gold and Rubén G. Rumbaut

A Series from LFB Scholarly

Latino Churches
Faith, Family, and Ethnicity in the Second Generation

Ken R. Crane

LFB Scholarly Publishing LLC
New York 2003

Library of Congress Cataloging-in-Publication Data

Crane, Ken R., 1957-
  Latino churches : faith, family, and ethnicity in the second
generation / Ken R. Crane.
     p. cm. -- (The new Americans)
  Includes bibliographical references and index.
   ISBN 1-59332-005-1 (alk. paper)
  1. Hispanic Americans--Religious life and customs. 2. Hispanic
American youth--Religious life and customs. 3. Hispanic
Americans--Ethnic identity. 4. Christianity and culture--United
States. I. Title. II. New Americans (LFB Scholarly Publishing LLC)
   BR563.H57C73 2003
   277.7'0829'08968--dc22

2003018748

ISBN 1-59332-005-1

Printed on acid-free 250-year-life paper.

Manufactured in the United States of America.

To my sister,
Diane Crane Iacopi

Table of Contents

Acknowledgements

"Without rich wanting, nothing arrives," wrote Carl Sandburg. Between the *wanting* and the *arrival* I was constantly dependant on other people. I thank my friend Edwin Hernández for sparking the desire to study religion among Latinos ("ken you must have *ganas*"). I gained much needed inspiration from friends and faculty at Michigan State University Department of Sociology, particularly Steven J. Gold (my dissertation Chair) and Rubén G. Rumbaut. Other members of my committee, Gene Burns and Brendan Mullan, gave extensive guidance along the way.

I wish to thank Jorge (*Jefe*) Chapa, Interim Director of The Julian Samora Research Institute for supporting research on the religious institutions of Latinos in the Midwest. The financial support provided by U.S.D.A. (Grant #97-36200-5207) enabled a critical phase of this research to move forward.

I was incredibly fortunate to come under the mentorship of anthropologist Ann Millard, whose guidance in ethnographic fieldwork methods was indispensable. I must also mention her husband Isidore Flores, a humorous and skilled focus group facilitator.

Additional fieldwork support was given by PARAL (Program for the Analysis of Religion among Latinos). In particular I want to thank PARAL Director Anthony (Tony) Stevens-Arroyo for valuable encouragement and feedback on earlier drafts of this manuscript.

Much thanks to those who read portions of the manuscript and gave helpful comments: Guillermo Martínez (also for his activism, music, and poet's ear); Father Flickenger; and ESL Coordinator Melanie Tijerina.

I owe much to many helpful people who gave invaluable advice and support along the way, and I will mention a few: Ramiro Reyes, Joe Marble, Bob Buttgen, Father Luis, Reverend Gutierrez, Sister Dolores, Rubén Cervantes, and Rebecca Waring.

Finally, to Alma, Roel, Daniel, Kristina, Ovidio, Abelardo, *Las Aguitas*, *Los Elegidos*—and so many others whose stories were the oxygen that breathed life into this book—*con alabanza!*

CHAPTER 1

Introduction

It is an ordinary Sunday morning on Bowne Street. A flock of Hindu worshippers parades down the avenue with the bust of an elephant-headed deity in tow. Half a block up, joyful music emerges from a storefront that serves as a Sikh *gurdwara*, and across the street, a member of a Chinese evangelical church mutters disapprovingly about the double-parking proclivities of the temple goers. At the Bowne Street Community Church, the Taiwanese who once worshipped in a back room of the church now make up half the congregation, and the Taiwanese clergyman, the Rev. Norman Chang, is now the senior pastor.[1]

At a time when religion has emerged, in the words of R. Stephan Warner, as a "vital expression of groups in an increasingly diverse society," my hope is that this work will increase our understanding of the place of ethnic and immigrant religion at the beginning of the twenty-first century. The earlier empirical work that has framed the study of immigrant religion in this century was inspired by a massive, largely European movement of people to this country around the turn of the twentieth century. Roughly a century later, the scholarship for a new theory of immigrant religion will have its raw material in the mosques, temples, storefront churches, and cathedrals of believers from not only Europe but East and South Asia, the Caribbean, Latin America, Africa, and the Middle East as well.

The fundamental differences between the two migrations (such as national origins, class, contexts of reception, and race) have become one premise for rethinking theories of assimilation and ethnicity. Given the wider spectrum of non-Christian and non-conventional persuasions among new immigrants, (e.g. Yemeni and Pakistani Moslems, Hindus, Keralite Christians, Korean Presbyterians, Mexican Pentecostals, and Jamaican Rastafarians), it is also likely that theories of immigrant religion will require a similar review.

Unfortunately researchers have vastly neglected the rapidly expanding religious universe of these groups.[2] It is the purpose of this research to not only add to others' attempts to redress this "scholarly discrimination," but to do so in a way that consciously integrates two intellectual currents --the sociology of immigrant adaptation, and the "new paradigm" for religious study in the United States. There have been few attempts to consciously connect the important new research on socio-economic outcomes for immigrants and their children with the discussion of how religious space in America is being "restructured to reflect a new socio-demographic, multicultural context" (Roof 1993: 155; Warner 1993).[3]

In the Midwest, traditionally seen as insulated from immigrant populations, the rapid growth of Latinos in the last decade (in many instances due to immigrants of Mexican origin) is having a dramatic impact on both religious and secular institutions. Latinos are forming their own Spanish speaking congregations, as well as joining established parishioners, "creating a multi-ethnic environment which poses challenges to established ways of doing religion...from Catholics to mainline Protestants, evangelicals and Pentecostals...houses of worship are becoming multilingual zones" (Niebuhr 1999). Throughout southwest Michigan and north-central Indiana (the geographical focus of this ethnography) the most visible Latino institutions are their churches, Catholic as well as a plethora of Protestant and sectarian denominations.

Historically the Latino church has played a crucial role of mediating between marginalized groups and the institutions of dominant society:

> In most neighborhoods, the community church represents the only institution owned and operated by the Latino community...The Latino church stands at the very center of the community: serving, enacting rituals of hope and meaning, transmitting values, enabling leadership, organization... motivating to transform personal and communal life, and inspiring an idealism for a better future (Hernández 1999a: 18).

"Among the nearly 31 million Latinos and Latinas in the United States today, religion is a particularly powerful wellspring of Latino identity, cultural cohesiveness and family and social organization" (Stevens-Arroyo 2000). As the "center of a living community" these congregations function as extended families (Diaz-Stevens 1993; Sullivan, 2000). Latino churches are important resource institutions that provide for not only spiritual but also practical needs, and can function as communities of resistance to larger threatening forces. One commonly finds in churches various programs have been established to deal with practical needs—jobs, shelter, food, furniture, and schooling and immigration papers.

Latino Christians in the United States (Catholics, mainline Protestants, Evangelicals, and Pentecostals) have forged their unique forms of spirituality by drawing on their experiences of struggle, migration, and community. They have developed liturgy, music, and worship services inspired by the rich cultural heritage of many regions and Latin peoples.

Catholic and mainline Protestant Latino congregations in particular have a long history in the United States. In the last quarter of the twentieth century they have challenged their fellow Christians to pursue issues of social justice towards "the strangers within our gates," greater inclusion in church structures, and to do right by the youth in barrio schools. Pentecostal and evangelical Latinos have begun to challenge their Anglo counterparts to a more rigorous adherence to biblical truth and appropriate lifestyle. Both strands of tradition will no doubt have a growing impact on their respective faith communities. As immigration from Latin America continues to swell their ranks, Latinos will have to deal with an increasing intra-group diversity of race, ethnicity, class, and religious emphasis.

R. Stephan Warner (1993) observed that dominant characteristic of religion in America today is the intense energy invested in the continuance of subcultural and doctrinal identity--in articulating distinctiveness. A few scholars in the U.S. have turned their attention toward understanding how religious identities play out among the new immigrants (e.g. Williams 1988, Rutledge 1992; Ebaugh and Chavetz 2000; Warner and Wittner 1998; Stevens-Arroyo et. al. 2002). Drawing on their work we can see how immigrant groups are using religious institutions to strategically define themselves in ways that enhance their legitimacy while simultaneously maintaining identity and socializing the second generation within a strong moral, religio-cultural framework.

"Indeed, the children of today's immigrants constitute the most consequential and lasting legacy of the new mass immigration to the United States," says Ruben Rumbaut, who has followed the lives of over 5000 youth over the last 8 years (Portes and Rumbaut 2001:18).[4] With a view toward understanding the long-term changes of immigrant congregations, the specific goal of my research is to look at the role they play in the lives of the second generation, or children of immigrant parents, in this case Latino youth of Mexican origin. Many congregations fail to retain many of the second generation. The question of what is happening to the second generation is one reason why some scholars have turned their attention toward understanding the interplay of religious and ethnic identities as these youth come of age in American society (e.g. Kurien 1998; Chai 1998; Bankston and Zhou 1998; Yang 2000; Alumkal 2003).

The Latino church, says Hernández "functions as a community of memory where the moral and cultural values of Latino heritage and traditions are maintained and transferred to new generations" (1995: 43). For youth who are coming of age in small Midwestern communities that lack significant residential enclaves the church may be the only place (outside of family) where a person meets face to face with those of similar cultural background, and where the language and other cultural symbols are publicly affirmed. As places where personal biography intersects the cultural system, religious congregations can be windows to catching a glimpse of how the second generation is experiencing life within particular communities.

This research focuses on the second-generation youth within three Latino congregations (Catholic, Adventist, and Assembly of God) in Michigan and Indiana. Its methodology is qualitative and ethnographic, involving an immersion into the communities, churches, and schools that form the social environment of these youth. In addition to participant observation it uses in-depth interviews and focus groups to explore in detail how these congregations shape the lives of their America-born youth.

Notes

[1]Somini Sengupta (New York Times, 11/7/99)

[2]This is due, in part, to the absence of religious content in census and immigration data sources.

[33]These include: The New Ethnic and Immigrant Congregations Project (NIECPR), which culminated in the collection of ethnographies of immigrant congregations, "Gatherings in Diaspora," (Warner and Wittner 1998); the Program for the Analysis of Religion among Latinos/as (PARAL), (Stevens-Arroyo, Goris, and Keysar 2002); the Religion, Ethnicity, and New Immigrants Research (RENIR) project in Houston (Ebaugh and Chafetz 2000); the Gateway Cities: Project on Religion and the New Immigrants.

[4]The number of children born in this country of at least one immigrant parent, and between the ages of 0-17 is between 5.8 and 7.7 million depending on if decimal generations (1.5 or 2nd generation, etc.) are included (Oropesa 1997).

CHAPTER 2

Selective Acculturation and Ethnic Congregations

The role of religion has historically had a central place in the scholarship of immigration. It was clearly demonstrated that religion provided a crucial institutional mechanism for 1) coping with the trauma and anomie of migration; 2) reestablishing community; 3) preserving cultural values and identity; and 4) negotiating societal acceptance (Hansen 1952; Herberg 1955; Gordon, 1964). Prior to migration it was their religious traditions that had provided the symbolic meaning so crucial (in the Durkheimian sense of 'mechanical solidarity') to their cohesive, communal life:

> Back home, the church (or synagogue) had been for most of the people the meaningful center of life, the repository of the sacred symbols of community existence. As soon as they touched land in the New World, they set themselves to re-establishing it (Herberg 1955: 11).

Ethnic congregations[1] in the United States have historically been a means in reclaiming *gemeinschaft*[2]--where intimate, close, face-to-face interaction with co-ethnics took place. "In the United States the (immigrant) churches came to serve an ethnic role; they helped sort out 'who one was' in a bewilderingly complex society" (Greeley 1972: 125). In the classic 'Yankee City' study by Warner and Srole (1945) the church was the primary organizer of ethnic groups as community systems. By providing the social space to maintain cultural traditions, churches and synagogues helped facilitate the formation of ethnic group identity.

Communities of Memory

As people leave behind family and the familiar, the immigrant experience continues to contain a sense of loss. The psychologist Ricardo Ainsley (1998) describes this process as "cultural mourning." As a natural component of this mourning process, immigrants make use of "linking objects" and "linking processes" that help sustain the sense of connection to that which was lost. Religious symbols (such as *Nuestra Señora de Guadalupe* for Mexican Catholics) become important symbols to sustain a connection to the world left behind. Applying Ainsley's concept to religious congregations means that they become important places that allow a lost world to be reconstructed and "vehicles for effective engagement" with the new world to emerge.

"The future is connected to the past by the slender thread of memory," observed Raymond B. Williams in his study of southern Asian immigrants in the U.S. (1988: 12). For many immigrants the religious congregation continues to be a community of memory. It may be the only place (outside of the family) where a person meets face to face with those of similar cultural background, and where cultural symbols are publicly affirmed. Ebaugh and Chafetz' description of immigrant religious groups in

Houston highlights this importance: "…religion is often at the center of immigrants' sense of identity and religious institutions serve as focal points for ethnic gatherings, celebrations and re-creations of ethnic language and customs…" (2000: 13).

The role of religious congregations as communities of memory in cultural affirmation and practical survival demonstrates its functional continuity. There are however a number of contextual factors that must be addressed in current studies of immigrant congregations. For example, many Mexican immigrants in the United States travel annually to Mexico and maintain the hope of eventual return (Chavez 1998). This raises the possibility that many of the Mexican communities of memory have transnational dimensions. For many immigrant groups today, the globalizing economy with its tele-communication networks facilitates intense "virtual" contact between individuals and communities in different parts of the world. This raises the possibility that transnationalism mediates the "cultural mourning" process (Ainsley 1998; Brittain 2002). Other contextual factors that may affect how the second-generation views the ethnic congregation, and whether Herberg's observations about the relationship between religion and ethnicity still hold within these new contexts, are addressed below.

Herberg's Thesis and the "New Immigration"

Will Herberg in *Protestant-Catholic-Jew* (1955) observed that the children of immigrants who arrived around the turn of the nineteenth century did not strongly identify with the ethnic group of its parents and this rejection was transferred to the immigrant church:

> Those who rejected their ethnic identification or felt uncomfortable in it transferred this rejection to the church and the religion of their immigrant parents. In revolting against the immigrant heritage, and in the process of establishing their independence and adjusting themselves to their new environment, they tended to cast off their religious identification. To them religion, along with the language of the home, seemed to be part and parcel of the immigrant baggage of foreignness they were so eager to abandon (p. 19).

The relationship identified by Herberg was that the declining significance of ethnicity among the immigrant second generation contributes towards a declining significance in the role of religion. For Herberg's thesis to have any theoretical merit today requires that one's religious and ethnic identities be still very closely linked. Phillip Hammond and K. Warner (1993) argue that the inroads of both assimilation and secularization have made the relationship between religious and ethnic identity much weaker than in the past, and predict the continuation of that trend. Such a conclusion means that Herberg's thesis will continue to have less explanatory relevance than in the past.

To explain how Hammond and K. Warner came to that conclusion requires us to review Abramson's (1980) taxonomy[3] of the three types of ethnic religion:

1) "ethnic fusion"--religion is the foundation of ethnicity (Jews, Hutterites, Amish);

2) "ethnic religion"--an ethnic group tends to be grounded in a relatively unique religion (Greek Orthodox, Dutch Reformed);

3) "religious ethnicity"--an ethnic group may be linked to a religious tradition, but religious identification can also be made outside of ethnic identification, (e.g. Polish, Irish, Italian Catholics).

In their study[4] they found Catholic Americans of European descent to be just as assimilated as Protestants, but less secular. They concluded that for Catholics religious identity helps to maintain ethnic identity more than ethnic identity helps to maintain religious identity. For Protestants however they found no clear pattern. Mexicans and African-American had much lower rates of either assimilation or secularization.

Based on these findings they make three generalizations that are relative to Herberg's thesis: (1) that "ethnic identification and loyalty to the religion of one's ethnic group have both tended to diminish in the American context," (2) processes of secularization and assimilation occur at a slower pace among ethnic groups regarded as minorities, (3) ethnic identity appears to decline before religious identity. Overall they conclude that as religion becomes more and more of an individual matter,[5] "ethnicity will have a declining effect in determining religious identity" (p. 66).

What Hammond and K. Warner meant by secularization was its declining *social* significance. The personal and psychological salience of religion may actually increase when it becomes more a matter of personal choice. Indeed religion is seen by the many rational choice theorists as an important matter for many *individuals* within a competitive religious marketplace (Iannaccone 1994). This view of religion reduces its significance to one of many commodities within a consumerist lifestyle characteristic of most Americans. In addition, we know that the dislocation associated with migration may increase the salience of religion, but for both psychological and collective reasons (maintenance of ethnic identity and resource mobilization).

Hammond and K. Warner conclude that "ethnicity will have a declining effect in determining religious identity" in the future (p. 66). This claim warrants further scrutiny since, if true, it would put to rest the usefulness of Herberg's thesis for the study of immigrant religion in America. For the purposes of this study of the second generation therefore, one could ask if we are seeing a fundamental difference in the relationship between ethnic and religious identity among the second generation? The fact that the minority respondents in Hammond and K. Warner's study resisted both secularization and assimilation raises another conceptual challenge to Herberg's thesis: are we seeing the emergence of ethnic religious institutions that may resist assimilation? Since the 1970s there has been mounting evidence that ethnic identification is made through religious institutions. Recent studies of the second generation reveal the existence and persistence of ethnic communities that support strong economic, educational and religious institutions, which facilitate a "selective" pattern of immigrant acculturation (Portes and Rumbaut 1996, 2001; Sullivan 2000). Furthermore, many new immigrants are forming religious congregations as *both* a strategy of accommodation and identity maintenance (Williams 1988; Rutledge 1993; Gold 1992; Kurien 1998; Hepner 1998; Alumkal 2003).

Is it appropriate to conclude, then, as do Hammond and K. Warner, that ethnicity will have less effect in determining religious identity? The basis of this assertion has to do with identity as an individualistic rather than group expression of *mechanical solidarity* as described by Durkheim ([1893] 1933). In an earlier study Hammond (1988) suggested that both the persistence of ethnic and religious identities is less an expression of group identity -- Durkheim's *collective conscience*--than an individualistic one compatible with a free market, or multicultural, system of voluntary involvements. The "collective expressive" involvement is "largely involuntary because it emerges out of overlapping primary group ties not easily avoided" (p. 6). The "individual expressive" mode of involvement "is largely voluntary and independent of other social ties" (p. 6). Such a conceptualization associates "collective expressive" with "immigrant", and "individual expressive" with assimilation of the second generation. (This does not take into account the kinds of acculturation that have already taken place before families and children emigrate.)

Despite the problems associated with this conceptualization it is still useful to consider whether the second generation tends to experience religion in more of an "individual expressive" versus a "collective-expressive" manner. Some research among evangelical Latino youth claims to support this hypothesis (Hernández and Dudley 1990). Others have identified patterns of assimilation, which embrace individualistic, consumerist choices that the religio-cultural preferences of the immigrant parents be rejected (Rumbaut 1994; Portes and Rumbaut 2001). In the AVANCE study Hernández (1995) found a weakening of some aspects of religious commitment among more highly acculturated Latino youth. The same data, however, also reveal continuities between the first and second generations that would have surprised Herberg, for example, that church attendance among the more "highly acculturated" was just as high as the "less acculturated" (Hernández 1995; Crane 1998). I would argue that the choices of many "highly acculturated" youth are still made in deference to the moral world of family and cultural group. The youth in tight-knit ethnic communities (such as the Vietnamese in Bankston and Zhou's study) clearly do not act in an "individual expressive" manner when it comes to religious involvement.

While immigrant congregations have historically fostered some kind of ethnic identity, it should be noted that within the racial thinking of early twentieth century United States ethnicity was conceded at best only a transitional status (Herberg 1955). The current affirmation of ethnic identity is a context that has clearly changed. In her study of Hindu religious organizations in California, Prema Kurien (1998) found that involvement in religious congregations were one mode by which the second generation honored ethnic identity and took its place "at the multicultural table" (see also Ebaugh and Chavetz 2000; Sullivan 2000; Alumkal 2003). One could still argue that the salience of ethnic identity reflects individual preferences within this climate of multiculturalism. However it should not matter whether ethnic identity is more a product of the collective expression of the group or of identity politics—it is the same in its *consequences*. For the Indian and Tamil youth in Kurien's study, honoring ones ethnicity, whether from collective or individual motivations, still resulted in some kind of involvement in the religion of their ethnic group—namely Hinduism.

It could be argued that religion may well be an important vehicle of ethnic expression, but that does not *ipso facto* give it social significance. I would argue, however, that in a culture increasingly preoccupied with identity and difference, and in the context of demographic change driven by immigration, the role of mediator of cultural difference gives religion great social significance. Further, while it is true that there may indeed be an erosion of some kind of communal (read national) life, religion has remained and increasingly become the center of many "communities" (congregations) of faith (Warner and Wittner 1998).

There is ample evidence therefore that situations exist where ethnicity and religion are closely linked, and hence Herberg's thesis may still be valid. There are some clear differences however between what Herberg saw happening and what we see presently in the relationships between ethnicity and religion. Herberg based his conclusions on the pattern of the second generation of his time, how the children of immigrants saw ethnic religion as an impediment to success in America, and moved "up and out," of their ethnic group into the Anglo mainstream. For the children and grandchildren of those immigrants who had largely rejected their parents' old country traditions, it was religious or denominational affiliation within the three main religions (the "transmuting pot" of Protestantism, Catholicism, and Judaism) that came to replace ethnicity as the salient marker of social location and identity.

In short while America knows no national or
cultural minorities except as temporary, transitional
phenomena, it does know a free variety and
plurality of religions; and it is as members of a
religious group that the great mass of Americans
identify themselves to establish their social location
once they have really sloughed off their immigrant
foreignness (p. 38).

Denominational identity (Catholic, Protestant, Jew)
gradually replaced ethnicity as the marker of social
location. Herberg concluded that ethnic identity was
merely transitional. Even when Hansen's (1938) principle
was operative ("what the son wishes to forget, the grandson
wishes to remember"), the attempt by the third generation
(grandchildren) to reconnect with their ethnic roots was no
longer viable—the immigrant culture had largely
disappeared. Today that is clearly not the case for many of
the second generation. Where ethnicity is celebrated by the
second generation it may very likely be through religious
institutions.   As Kurien suggests, the constant
replenishment of new first generation immigrants of many
groups means that children and even grandchildren will
encounter a thriving immigrant culture. For second
generation Latinos experiencing a resurgence of ethnic
identification, reintegration may be sought within a
religious institution (Hernández 1999).

Another different and unique situation presently exists
that was not addressed by earlier theorists. Many of the
second generation are members of sectarian and
fundamentalist religious subcultures (e.g. Pakistani and
Yemeni Moslems, Latino Pentecostals, etc.), which adhere
to an all-encompassing belief system that transcends ethnic

boundaries (e.g. Islam).   Lack of empirical data about these emerging groups prevents us from drawing any conclusions about their implications for Herberg's thesis (but see Hernández 1995; Jacobson 1997).   One empirical study, although from Great Britain, may be useful in understanding dynamics in the United States as well. Jessica Jacobson (1997) found that for young British Pakistanis, religious identity had much greater salience than their ethnic identity. These youth differentiated between their ethnic and religious identities along two fronts: culture and origins.   In terms of religio-ethnic culture, young British Pakistanis spoke disparagingly of how Pakistani culture, by synthesizing a variety of non-orthodox practices into its form of Islam, had diluted its purity. They called for a purer form of Islam without the syncretism of their immigrant parents.[6] In terms of religio-ethnic origins they were critical of nationalistic distinctions and emphasized their Muslim identity.

Furthermore she found that the ethnic and religious boundaries defined and maintained by these youth were substantially different in levels of salience. The boundaries defining expressions of ethnic identity were "semi-permeable", i.e. were "easy to cross in most social situations, and don't act to insulate or isolate the ethnic minority from the diverse influences of wider society" (p. 247). The religious boundaries in contrast were "pervasive and clear cut," evoked in a "concrete and unequivocal manner," and permeated the everyday interactions and activity with religious meaning (p. 248).   This reflects Islam's claim to present universal truth for all of humanity. For these youth it was their religion, Islam, with its universal relevance and applicability that established more clearly their place in the world, rather than ethnicity, which was more situational and related to a particular people and place.

But Islam is not the only religion that makes claims to universal truth and maintains rigid boundaries that are evoked in the minutia of everyday life.   Similar observations have been made about sectarian congregations in the U.S. and their immigrant counterparts. For some Latino Protestant sects religious identity is invoked frequently and everything in life is fraught with religious significance--drinking habits, dress, holidays (Hernández 1996; León 1998; Sullivan 2000).   These religious subcultures may stand independent of ethnic subcultures, and cultural norms may be rejected or accepted according to one's religious ideology.

The examples above are interesting because they put Herberg's thesis on its head--religious adherence leads to a decline in ethnic significance.   Herberg's thesis is less useful for these situations, since religious identity stands more independent of ethnic identity, but for the opposite reason than that proffered by Hammond and K. Warner (fundamentalism and religious resurgence versus secularization).

COMMUNITIES OF ENGAGEMENT--ETHNIC ASSERTION AND ACCOMMODATION

In his introduction to an ethnography of Orthodox Jewish communities, Lynn Davidman (1991) says that all religious groups in the United States make some kind of accommodation—"adapting certain features of the religion to make it more consonant with secular ways of life" (p. 32).   On the other hand Ainsley (1998) argues that the cultural mourning process, as it publicly affirms cultural symbols, also leads to engagement with the host society. It is not surprising then that immigrant congregations are places where both accommodation and assertion may be taking place (Smith 1978; Gold 1992).

Raymond B. Williams, writing about Hindu communities observed that "In the United States, religion is the social category with clearest meaning and acceptance in the host society, so the emphasis on religious affiliation and identity is one of the strategies that allows the immigrant to maintain self-identity while simultaneously acquiring community acceptance" (Williams 1988: 11). How do ethnic religious organizations, as they make congregational adaptations, serve to maintain identity in American society? Several examples demonstrate the often unexpected ways in which identity is negotiated.

In her ethnography of two Hindu Indian organizations in Los Angeles, Prema Kurien, (1998) tells how "becoming Hindu" was a way to make the transition from "sojourners to citizens." Both the Organization of Hindu Malayalees (OHM) and BalaVihar (Child Development group for Tamils) were formed out of a collective desire to preserve their heritage, find community, and pass on their values to the second generation. They resemble American religious congregations by holding study and discussion groups (analogous to "Sunday Schools") and provide programs that meet a broad spectrum of emotional and physical needs. The organizations help to mark identity -- they have "become the key symbol of identity and of difference from American society." (p. 64). However this difference is packaged in a way that non-Indians understand--through religion--thus legitimizing an Indian-American identity. They function further as articulators of

Hindu culture in response to negative stereotypes about Indians.

For communal continuity they are critical because they are the primary vehicle of socialization of the second generation into an "Indian-American identity." "Sunday School" programs of the BalaVihar often draw on Hindu sacred texts and poetry or drama, and discussion groups deal with Indian culture and religion. This allows both acceptance and maintenance of identity. An Indian-American identity is negotiated from a position of communal strength through an organization that has a strong pride and commitment to its way of life and worldview. The presence of strong religious organizations provides the vehicle for Hindu Indians in Americans to take their place "at the multicultural table" (Kurien 1998: 45; see also Williams 1988).

For the Vietnamese in California the establishment of Buddhist Pagodas[7]) was a particularly effective means of preserving and teaching important communal values (Gold 1992). Gold described how in the resettlement era Buddhist leaders provided a critique of American society while working toward a future that would include a synthesis of East and West (p. 192). Rutledge (1992) describes how religion becomes the "bridge" the Vietnamese use to "walk back and forth between the two contact cultures. More recent ethnographies describe how Vietnamese religious congregations continue to absorb aspects of the contact culture without losing the key aspects of ethnic identity (Huynh 2000; Kwon 2003).

In summary, the religion of immigrants has involved certain accommodations that enhanced their legitimacy (adopting familiar organizational, congregational styles), while at the same time finding the cultural space to maintain identity and strategically define themselves. They have, as Gold observed about the Vietnamese in California, been "involved in a complex style of adaptation to American society" that included both cultural preservation and the acceptance of mainstream practices. (In Woldemikael's terminology, they 'synthesized assertion and accommodation,' quoted in Gold 1992: 226). They have also, as Kurien illustrated, through the formation of ethnic religious congregations articulated their religion in ways well understood traditionally by most Americans, and in the process developed vehicles aimed to reproduce ethnicity.

Religious Institutions and Ethnic Socialization

It is the question of how immigrant congregations go about socializing the second generation within a strong moral, religio-cultural framework that we now turn. It is important here that we recognize the array of competing forces that beset children of immigrants. These are well illustrated in both research and literary narratives:

> Relative to both the first and third generations, the process of ethnic self-identification of second-generation children is more complex, and often entails the juggling of competing allegiances and attachments. Situated within two cultural worlds, they must define themselves in relation to multiple reference groups (sometimes in two countries and in two languages) and to the classifications into which they are placed by their foreign-born parents, native peers, schools, the ethnic community and the larger society. Pressure from peers and from parents can

tighten the tug-of-war of ethnic and national loyalties, contributing unwittingly to a sense of marginality (Portes and Rumbaut 2001: 150).

The marginality referred to by Portes and Rumbaut comes from not being fully accepted or understood by ones own ethnic group (being called *gringa* or *white bread* by more recent immigrants) nor by dominant society ("spic go home" written on the lunch table), or parents' restrictions that embarrass them.   Attempting to negotiate both worlds, they fail to find a sense of full belonging that reduces anxiety about ones identity.

The ways in which the second generation resolves questions of identity and makes its way in American society are varied and complex, and recent research has generated new conceptual models that challenge traditional concepts of "assimilation." The concept of "segmented assimilation" (Portes and Zhou 1993; Rumbaut 1994; Portes and Rumbaut 2001) attempts to describe a process or pattern emerging in the studies[8] of children of the "new" immigration. These "multiple and contradictory" paths are in fact adaptations to various class and racial subsystems of society (hence the term "segmented"), that ultimately reflect social and economic outcomes in adulthood--school performance, occupational attainment, and involvement in risk behaviors and deviance. The frequencies of adaptation are clustered around four types of acculturation: (1) *consonant acculturation*, in which parents and children acquire English and cultural competency in similar fashion, which can mean "Americanization"[9] or straight-line assimilation into the dominant culture, or alternatively lead to (2) *consonant resistance*, where parents and children isolate themselves from the host society, (3) *dissonant acculturation*, in which parents and children go different directions culturally, experiencing a rupture of family ties and often involvement in *adversarial subcultures*, (4) *selective acculturation*, involving a preservation of parental authority and cultural values, higher rates of bilingualism, and usually upward mobility, (Portes and Zhou 1993; Portes and Rumbaut 2001). These patterns are shaped along the way by a number of socio-demographic or "toponomical" factors, including social and economic capital, family dynamics, geographical location, spatial concentration, context of reception and societal reaction (Fernández Kelly and Shauffler 1996[10]; Portes and Zhou 1993; Rumbaut 1994; Portes and Rumbaut 2001).

Ethnic Socialization and Selective Acculturation

Selective acculturation is a mode of adjustment in which parents and children in immigrant families acculturate in similar directions and retain traditional values and language (Hurh and Kim 1984; Portes and Rumbaut 1996). As Portes and Rumbaut (1994) explain, acculturation occurs along a continuum. At one end is where "generational dissonance" occurs because a highly acculturated second generation is not guided by the parents, and parents' lack of language skills requires them to depend on their children to deal with the outside world. Dissonant acculturation is associated with "loss of parental authority and role reversal, rupture of family ties and children's abandonment of the ethnic community" (p. 243). At the other end is where generational consonance occurs, because both generations acculturate at roughly the same rate and with encouragement from the immigrant community. The integration and linguistic acculturation of the immigrant generation prevents role reversal. Some aspects of selective acculturation such as bilingualism are highly correlated with increased psychosocial well-being (Portes and Rumbaut 2001).[11]

Another description of the same phenomenon is that of "adhesive adaptation" described by Kim and Hurh (1993) in their studies of the acculturation patterns of Koreans. The noted how Korean immigrants could "adhesively attach certain forms of American identity to the existing ethnic identity" (p. 5). Such "adhesive identities" reflect a growing desire (and ability) to hold American and ethnic identities simultaneously. Yang in his study of Chinese Christians in America (1999) found that some of the most effective members and leaders were those who were able to add multiple identities (Chinese, American, Christian) together without losing any single one. They had fluency in several languages (including several Chinese languages) both cultures, and the religious culture.

There are two essential features in the process of selective acculturation, both involving the ethnic community: (1) The ethnic community is the primary socializer of youth, and (2) it has the social capital to effect upward mobility of the succeeding generations. Documented examples are Punjabis in California (Rumbaut 1995; Gibson 1991), Vietnamese communities in New Orleans and California (Bankston and Zhou 1998; Gold 1992) and Cubans in south Florida (Portes and Zhou 1993).

Bankston and Zhou (1998) have given us a detailed examination of the mechanisms of socialization within Vietnamese communities. First the Vietnamese community is highly mobilized for cooperation, and has evolved further into a mechanism for social control:

... the dense, multiplex social system of family or kinship ties, religious ties, organizational ties and work ties weaves its members into a fabric of both supports and controls that is in many ways conducive to successful adaptation to American society (p. 222).

This, combined with a high degree of consensus of communal norms, produces a buffer against "negative" influences. Therefore the community is able to exert itself to become the primary *socializer* of the individual into American society, or negotiates incorporation into larger society on more acceptable terms. Those who have been socialized by the community experience upward mobility without the "straight-line" pattern of assimilation.

The authors claim that without the buffer of the strong ethnic community, immigrant parents would be powerless to protect their children from the "oppositional subculture" of the "immediate social environment" (p. 224). Since "bad kids" are shunned from the community, they are not subjected to traditionally effective group affirmation and sanction (the "Vietnamese microscope"). Vietnamese youth therefore tend to take a bifurcated path, clustering around very good or very bad outcomes.

Overall, the ability to make strategic and selective accommodations without assimilation in the traditional sense, that leads to "selective acculturation" of the second generation, is fostered by strong generational ties, strong ethnic institutions, community affirmation of both individual and family, in general adequate "moral and material resources" and a "well integrated" ethnic community that can exercise considerable influence over the second generation (Portes and Rumbaut 1996).

Selective Acculturation and Religio-cultural Institutions

In his study of Vietnamese communities in Oklahoma City, Rutledge (1992) found that the Vietnamese first generation immigrant elders and parents were disturbed by the rapid Americanization of their youth, and employed religious involvement (both Buddhism and Catholicism) as a means to counter the trend. Innovations were made to "emotionally and intellectually better incorporate the youth into a Vietnamese way of life" (p. 67).

In a similar fashion Korean churches, alarmed at the large exodus of their college age youth (estimates of 90% according to Chai 1998), has explicitly committed itself to maintenance of cultural values through its Korean language and cultural classes. It is common to find Korean churches operating a thriving well-attended Korean School staffed with teachers who in some cases are trained in Korea but unable to teach in the American system. There are weekly Korean language classes held for children of all ages through high school. They are often specifically targeted for children born in the U.S. who have become more proficient in English than Korean. Besides language, other cultural traditions are taught, such as Tae Kwon Do (see Chai 1998).

What we have learned from the Vietnamese community, however, is that such strategies are only effective if they work to integrate youth into the ethnic community. Kurien's study of Indian youth revealed that language barriers prevented youth from participating fully in the religious congregations that utilized native languages. The Houston RENIR study (Ebaugh and Chafetz 2000) also found that while language and education are potential sources of cultural transmission, they do not necessarily influence or retain the second generation. What many churches (particularly Korean and Chinese) have done is to adopt English services and programs to serve the second generation (Chai 1998; Yang 1999).

Bankston and Zhou found that it was the social network fostered by ethnic churches that was more important in cultural maintenance than language classes. For Vietnamese High School students, church attendance was a strong predictor of the maintenance of intergenerational Vietnamese identity churches because it provided a significant link to co-nationals. Church attendance had a positive impact on social adjustment (grades, aspirations for college, and rates of substance abuse) even when controlling for background variables such as time lived in the U.S. Much of this positive effect however may have been due to the ethnic identification facilitated by church involvement. Instead of limiting opportunities for "successful" adjustment to American life, strong ethnic identification in the context of religious community enables youth to have higher levels of academic achievement and avoid certain risk behaviors associated with youth culture. This suggests that the religious involvement of immigrant children can indeed facilitate outcomes associated with selective acculturation.

Ethnic religion, by providing a locus of networking, is one of the mechanisms by which ethnic communities reproduce their values in the next generation. It is clear that in the Vietnamese and South Asian examples, religion is part of the web of relationships that exert themselves on youth, the others being family strong kinship and social networks and ethnic organizations.

These examples however do not necessarily tell us whether the second generation finds religious institutions helpful in resolving the psycho-social tensions of negotiating the worlds of parents and peers, as referred to earlier by Portes and Rumbaut. Many ethnic congregations (Latinos being an exception) resorted to English language programs to retain the second generation. The case of the Korean immigrants is noteworthy because it shows that the second generation found it necessary to form an English language, semi-autonomous church around those who shared the common experience of being both Korean and American in order to resolve its identity issues.

Latino youth on the other hand have not marked out space in the religious sphere that differentiates themselves from parents and grandparents, where, like Korean Americans, they can find expression with those primarily of the second generation. Latino clergy (see chapters 5 and 6) generally find it inconceivable that youth would not be at the same services their parents attend (in contrast to Korean-American youth). There are exceptions, however, and some Latino clergy are innovating with English services to retain the second generation.[12] This suggests that congregations under the influence of immigrant parents and clergy are struggling to cope with a generation that is coming to terms with American society in a way uniquely different from their own. They fear that youth will fall into bad company. The youth, having forged bilingual identities incorporating elements of both Latino and Anglo culture, likewise struggle to be understood on their own terms:

> Its not our fault that we don't have that [parents] culture in us...they would speak about terms that everybody was supposed to understand, and you

don't understand it because you weren't a part of that you were part of big macs, french fries, and you know. That ('s) what you can relate to...I think they [clergy] should understand also our culture, the fact that some of us were born and raised here and we're more Americanized than they would be....[13]

These sentiments reveal that the second generation in Latino congregations is struggling with issues of acceptance and relevancy. Some feel they are excluded from leadership; they interpret religious programs as attempts by clergy to control them (Sullivan 2000). This suggests that it is vital to understand more about how the Latino second generation is experiencing these congregations. It is not clear whether the powerful integrative effects found by Bankston and Zhou in Vietnamese congregations are at work in Latino congregations.

THE RESEARCH QUESTION

The primary question of this research is "Do Latino congregations facilitate outcomes associated with selective acculturation among the second generation?" If they do, then we would see signs that this is taking place, such as bilingualism and high levels of cultural consonance between generations. To facilitate the path of selective acculturation means that congregations are able to reinforce parental efforts to transmit cultural values of the ethnic community to the second generation; and therefore have influence on their worldview (ultimate values and existential postulates). Specific indicators of this are whether youth identify with the ethnicity of parents, and agree to a large extent with the cultural values of their parents about such matters as religious involvement, family relationships, and popular culture.

It is not clear what proportion of the second generation have chosen to leave these congregations. Hopefully by understanding the experiences of the youth who have chosen to remain will give us some clues as to why some have left—although that is beyond the scope of this study.

A number of subthemes will also be explored: (1) What explains the present attachment of the second generation, and what can we say about their future involvement? (2) Does the ethnic congregation have a different influence over second and first generation youth? Does it mean different things for them? For example is the ethnic congregation a place of comfort to the first generation youth, but a stifling and rigid environment for the second generation? (3) Do Protestant and Catholic congregations shape the lives of their youth differently?

A final subtheme explores the similarities and differences between the effects of these churches on their members and the historical role of immigrant churches in the U.S. as described by Herberg and Hansen. *Do we see a fundamental difference in how the second generation approaches the ethnic or immigrant church today?* Finally, what are their similarities and differences between the congregations of this study and those of other research initiatives (particularly those of NIECPR, RENIR, PARAL, Gateway Cities)?

Congregations are "living communities" where the second generation is being shaped by the parental generation and the cultural system of the church and ethnic group. It is also "living" in the sense that it is defining its own identity and place within the ethnic community and society at large. What follows in the next section is a description of the ethnographic methods employed to understand how the ethnic church is shaping the lives of its American-born youth.

Notes

[1]The term ethnic congregation is not necessarily synonymous with "immigrant congregation" although many of its members may be foreign born; I use the term "ethnic" to refer to a congregation whose religious expression reflects the language and culture of a particular group in the United States whose existence may be longstanding (Latino, Serbian, Chinese), or recent (Haitian, Rastafarian, Mayan).

[2]Germans still use the word *Gemeinder* for religious congregations, which has the same etymological root as *Gemeinschaft*.

[3]Hammond and K. Warner's terminology is in quotations.

[4]The respondents were mostly of European origin, all either Protestant or Catholic, with a small number of African- Americans and Hispanics.

[5]This line of reasoning is consistent with "supply-side" trends in the study of American religion that stress the marketplace dynamics of individual choice and government regulation.

[6]The British film "My Son the Fanatic" gives an excellent cinematic portrayal of this salience of religious over ethnic identity.

[7]At the time of his study Gold reported the existence of 39 pagodas.

[8]Prominent data sources for these conclusions have been the *Children of Immigrants: The Adaptation Process of the Second Generation* (CILS), a longitudinal study conducted in South Florida and Southern California by Portes and Rumbaut et. al.; Mary Waters' study of West Indian youth in New York; Min Zhou and Carl Bankston III's study of Vietnamese youth in New Orleans.

[9]The term acculturation has been used in the past to describe a step within a desired trajectory of assimilation into the dominant Anglo-Saxon layer of society (Gordon 1964). That is not way the term acculturation should be understood in this document, but rather as part of an adjustment process that may involve resistance to assimilative pressures.

[10]Fernández Kelly and Schauffler illustrate further nuances of segmentation with a typology of five immigrant groups: Nicaraguan

Sliders, Cuban Gainers, Haitian Strivers, Mexican Toilers, Vietnamese Bystanders.

[11]The same study concludes that bilingualism was also associated with better school performance.

[12]There are a growing number of Latino churches that are experimenting with English services to retain second-generation youth.

[13]Source is transcript from focus group of Puerto Rican youth conducted by sociologist Edwin Hernández, for the AVANCE study (Hernández 1995).

CHAPTER 3

Fieldwork Methods

The Nature of this Study

This research ethnographically explores the social and religious experiences of Latino youth (the second generation of Mexican origin[1]) within their faith communities in order to answer the question "Do Latino congregations facilitate outcomes associated with selective acculturation among the second generation?" There is more than one way one could seek answers to this question. I have chosen to examine how these particular youth, as they are coming of age in rural Midwestern communities, *experience* the ethnic church—"what happens when their lives intersect the subcultural systems of the ethnic church?" The inspiration for this focus on *experience* comes from the tradition of phenomenology, the Weberian notion of *Verstehen*, and the "interprepretive" mode of "thick description" (Geertz 1973).

To understanding then how the second-generation experiences the ethnic church requires being able to see and grasp the world from their perspective. While the goal of any ethnography is to see the world through the eyes of others, most fieldworkers recognize the limited authority of their voice. This impossibility for ethnographers to entirely "inhabit" the minds of those they seek to understand, is according to James Clifford a "perennial dilemma" for ethnographers (qtd. in Davidman 1991). Some attempts to mitigate my own bias included giving portions of my manuscript to respondents and key informants to read and react to, and sharing my findings with scholars who are from the same ethnic community as those I studied.

How people enact meaning through religion does not happen in a vacuum, but (in part) represents responses to life situations of a particular historical epoch and social climate. I have made an effort to understand how the transcendent meaning systems of a religion are "shaped by the opportunities and pressures of the larger social context" (Davidman 1991: 31). Throughout the ethnographic portrayals of people and events I have continually sought to find windows into wider structural and cultural processes that are shaping communities—an attempt to find the macro within the often mundane of the micro.

My choice of ethnography[2] as a method is influenced by the fact that it has produced some of the most definitive work to date on ethnic and immigrant religion and the second generation (for example, Warner and Wittner 1998; Yang 1999; Ebaugh and Chavetz 2000). Ethnography has also proved useful in numerous other social phenomena, such as the reproduction of class (Willis 1977; McCloed 1995), gender and migration (Grasmuck and Pessar 1991; Hondognue-Sotelo 1996). This suggests that ethnographic research principles are useful in understanding religious and ethnic subculture--the meaning systems, rituals and boundaries--of ethnic congregations and their related social linkages and networks. Researchers have pointed out the need for ethnographic studies where deeper, cultural phenomena are the focus of inquiry (Rumbaut 1997). A recent study of the role of the ethnic church in the social adjustment of Vietnamese youth suggests that "in depth" qualitative research could be particularly useful in

understanding the dynamics of growing up American.
(Bankston and Zhou 1996). Gold's ethnography of
Vietnamese cultural institutions in California did exactly
that, in portraying the "complex style of adaptation to
American society that included both cultural preservation
and the acceptance of dominant practices" (Gold 1992:
226).

As Michael Buroway (1991) points out, methodology
goes beyond pure technique to *link* data and theory. The
following pages explain how I collected and analyzed data
to deal with the research questions outlined earlier.

"I am the research instrument..."

Since every researcher has a peculiar set of characteristics
that emanate from him/her, it is important to try as much as
possible to be aware of how one might be influencing the
research process. This is not to focus on my limitations;
rather it is to help understand the inter-subjectivity of each
encounter. For example, the Catholic priest and
anthropologist Michael Lewis (1993) in his study of
Rastafarians did not stress the limitations that his being a
priest (and Caucasian) contained. While it presented some
unique challenges (Rastafarians understand the Pope as the
directing force behind 'Babylon' and continually called for
his renunciation of Catholicism), he saw his person as
eliciting certain questions and responses, and thus it
became part of the research task to be aware of what kind
of insight might emerge out of such tension.

In my case, being white and male has inevitably
influenced how people respond to my questions in a way
that has been, I believe, both advantageous *and* negative.
On the one hand I am sure it has resulted in a certain degree

of deference not granted to others. This has meant a certain degree of distance as well. On occasion I perceived some suspicion and concern about my trustworthiness, although this usually diminished over time.

Being male required tact in dealing with women, both married and single. I tried to avoid complications in this area by intentionally arranging interviews with women when their spouses were present, or in public settings (for example the quiet corner of the classroom, in an office with door left open, sitting in church after mass with others around, or at the counter during slow moments at the store).

My language skills allowed for casual conversation with non-English speakers, but were inadequate for conducting interviews. This did not present a serious obstacle to conducting research since my primary interest was with second-generation youth who were bilingual. During church services that were in Spanish I usually had someone translate portions that I did not understand. In conversations with parents or Spanish-only youth I availed the services of whoever was around to translate. Actually my willingness to try a converse with people at a primary level led to feelings of respect, goodwill, and (always) humor (my Spanish, of course, being the primary object of that humor).

There were several bridges of commonality that were to my advantage. One was my church membership (described below, which worked in my favor for one of the three congregations). The other was that most of these youth had grown up in the United States (and in the Midwest), which meant we did have at least some common cultural frames of reference.

Common to postmodern ethnography is an explanation of the nature of the relationship to those individuals and institutions with which one is conducting research. The three religious congregations have required different types of relationships. Having grown up in the Adventist tradition, and as a former administrator and teacher in the denomination, my relationship with the members of *Iglesia Adventista* had in insider quality to it—I was *hermano* (*brother* in the faith) Crane. I benefited from the trust that member status provides in a small, sectarian group. Many of the members were also related to one another, exaggerating the existing informality and familial atmosphere common to a small, rural congregation. This relaxed setting made it possible to break down walls of suspicion much faster than usual.

Because of my ongoing interest in Latino congregations (see Crane 1998) I had begun paying visits to the church in the winter of 1998. During one of those visits I met the pastor and explained my interest in doing research in his church at some point in the future. When that community became one of the study sites for the Julian Samora Research Institute[3] (JSRI) my visits became more frequent and my presence became more common. I explained to the pastoral staff the nature of the research and simply started attended services.

My status as a researcher probably had some degree of *liminality* since my *master status* continued to be *hermano*. During one visit to a family's home, for example, they expected me to first spent an hour in *culto* (study and prayer) before asking me if I was there for any other purpose (I proceeded to conduct my interview). That they carried on with their usual routine without making me the object of particular concern was an indicator that I had earned a certain level of familiarity and trust, which I consider to have enhanced the subsequent interview.

As for the Catholic parish, my relationship to the members there was much more inconspicuous given its size. I approached both the current and former parish priest to inform them of the study, and both welcomed me and gave helpful introductions to others. This led to relationships with some key individuals who have been important leaders in the Latino community.

For individuals within the Catholic congregation, my status as graduate assistant with JSRI has been a significant factor in peoples' openness to what I was doing (despite my being an "other" both in a religious and cultural sense). This could have to do with the church's much more intentional identification with Mexican culture, and the political activism of some members. I suspect that my involvement with JSRI probably overrode any hesitation on the part of lay leaders to devote generous amounts of time to my numerous questions, follow-up interviews, lunch meetings, and after-mass conversations.

My relationship with the Pentecostal congregation, Templo Rey began in a high school where I conducted several interviews and focus groups of students, many of whom were active in the church. When I began visiting prayer meetings and youth groups I was quickly accepted in my research role, since some of the members had already known me in that capacity at school. In addition I was welcomed by Pastor Cervantes, who was himself quite active in the community.

In addition to the congregations, I also conducted research at two high schools. This consisted of observing English as a Second Language (ESL) classes and interviewing students both individually and in focus groups. At Ciderville High I came to know the Coordinator of the ESL and Alternative Education Program who provided an office to conduct interviews and was very cooperative. At Meyerton High I spent time in participant observation, interviews with teachers and students, and three focus groups. An English teacher whom I met through the former mayor became a key informant and facilitated introductions with the administration. After a meeting during which I presented the research agenda I was given unquestioned access to observe and interview students. The level of openness and cooperation there was particularly impressive.

Level of Analysis—Youth in Community

This is a study of "youth in community." It seeks to understand these youth as they exist within their social worlds. A basic principle to ethnography is that research must seek to understand peoples within their natural socio-cultural setting, since "realities are wholes that cannot be understood in isolation from their contexts." (Lincoln and Guba 1985: 39). The significance to the research task of these contexts should not be underestimated.

The first social context under consideration is the religious congregation. Congregations are "local, face to face religious assemblies...living communities where we can observe what faith communities do for themselves, rather than what is stated by public relations spin doctors and official creeds" (Warner and Wittner 1998: 9). As "living communities" they are places where one can observe at the micro level what second generation Latino youth are doing for themselves, how they are expressing their own religious identity. They are places to observe the interaction between religion and ethnicity, and how this shapes the lives of youth.[4] The ethnic congregation also serves as the incubator for social networks that reinforce cultural values--including family and community institutions. As such it is an important linkage to family and friendship networks also, both crucial components of a person's "lifeworld."

However, to determine how the religious community shapes lives requires that we understand more about what is happening to people within the wider institutional matrix of family, school, peer group, and community. The wider community is also a place to observe how of different groups interact, and how Latinos participate in its institutions such as schools and labor markets. It is here that we learn more about the "macro" within the world of micro-interaction. It is for this reason that two high schools were included in the study. An ESL class and study hall were made accessible to observe and talk to Latino students. These students were later included in two focus group interviews.

What follows below is a detailed description of my qualitative techniques. This will include how certain individuals and institutions were chosen, the number of participants, and a brief profile of their social characteristics. This is followed by a description of how the data was organized and analyzed.

ETHNOGRAPHIC METHODS

I chose to focus my observation and interaction on the lives of two or three youth and their families in each congregation in order to understand their experience in greater depth. Below I have outlined the specific ethnographic, qualitative methods used to understand their lives and study what was happening both at the congregational level as well as the other social worlds of school and peer groups.

Participant Observation

I attempted to enter into the life of the youth by participating in and observing the ritual and enactment of meaning that took place at religious services and youth meetings. After-church potlucks and food sales were particularly fruitful occasions for more informal and informative conversations. Eventually I came to interact regularly with a smaller number families and individuals, with whom I would visit in their homes, offices, farms, and businesses. During this time I was involved in an interagency council that served farmworkers in southwest Michigan. Several individuals on that council were also church members.

I also immersed myself into the communities beyond the congregation. Several venues were particularly good for meeting people and getting a feel for the flow of life-- the *taqueria* (grill) in the back of a large *tienda mexicana* (Mexican shop), at the front counter of another *tienda*, the editor's office of the newspaper (for local gossip), several parks (weather permitting), and McDonalds (only because some youth worked there).

At Meyerton High School I spent about ten hours over a period of two months observing the high school study hall and talking in great depth to the ESL Coordinator and the Bilingual Tutor. This setting provided a rare opportunity to observe and interact with Latino students, many of whom were involved in area churches.

In-depth Interviews

In order to gain a deeper, more detailed documentation of youth experiences and the perspectives of significant others in their social networks, in-depth interviews were conducted. These included family members, teachers, clergy, lay leaders, business people, and program administrators. The ethnicity of most of these was Mexican-origin. Over half were between the ages of 15 and 25. Although I interviewed over 50 individuals, I eventually narrowed my focus to a smaller number of youth in each congregation (see Appendix 1 for profile of interview respondents).

The questions were loosely structured around nine primary areas (see Appendix B for sample questionnaire):

1) <u>life history</u>: individual and family history, birthplace of parents,_migration history, context of origin and reception, socio-economic backgrounds of family members, educational and occupational achievements.

2) <u>Identity</u>: how do they identify themselves, how significant is ethnic heritage (includes language use).

4) <u>religious participation</u>: extent of involvement in church and activities, the meaning to them of church involvement (phenomenological, interpretive dimensions).

5) <u>involvement in ethnic organizations:</u> voluntary organizations, formal or informal activities that serve ethnic solidarity, or function as cultural resources (social capital).

6) <u>social network</u>: who are significant friends, mentors, extended family?

7) <u>social adjustment</u>: attitude and performance toward school and other public institutions, feeling of acceptance by peers and wider community, employment experiences.

8) <u>inter-generational relationships</u>: how do youth feel about parent's ethnic heritage? Do parents criticize youth for being too American?

9) <u>the future</u>: plans, aspirations, career and educational goals.

The interview questions were open-ended, and additional time was spent on those items that evoked interesting responses. Follow-up interviews and informal conversations allowed for deeper probing of answers that were unclear or especially provocative.

Focus Groups

I felt that focused, group interviews could also reveal something useful. Three focus groups were conducted, with assistance from Dr. Ann Millard (an anthropologist) and her husband Isidore Flores, (a social psychologist). The first two were at Meyerton High School, and were primarily for understanding the Latino student experiences within the school system and community. One group was primarily Mexican-born, first generation. The second were mostly second generation, raised in the Midwest, who we nicknamed the "old timers." These both lasted over two hours, and included eight to ten students. After the focus group with the "old timers" ended several hung around to talk and eat for another one and a half to two hours (this probably had more to do with the classes they were missing than with our charisma). It was during our interview with this group that we made an important discovery—the amount of time they spent talking about their church experiences made us aware that their religious community had been extremely significant and formative in their lives.

A third focus group was conducted at St. Barbara's Catholic Church, with mostly second-generation youth of Mexican origin. The questions posed to this group focused more narrowly on questions of religious experience. All focus groups were taped and transcribed, with notes taken by an assistant that summarized people's statements.

Secondary Data Sources

There were some sources of data that provided useful background information, mostly newspapers at the town library, church periodicals, school newsletters, and census data.

Data Analysis and Coding

The organization of data has been done using a *grounded theory* approach (Strauss 1987). Central to this is the idea that qualitative analysis is not something that is done in some linear sequence, but is ongoing. The usefulness of this is perhaps best articulated by Becker (1986) observation that most hypotheses are developed *during* the analysis rather than *before* it. This requires a constant scrutiny of the data with a view of refining or adding certain questions. During my fieldwork I looked for certain questions which received fairly consistent answers (saturation), and I gradually moved from those to areas that required more clarification and elaboration.

The interview transcripts, field notes, and secondary data (hereon called texts) were coded using the *Outline of Cultural Materials* developed by Murdoch et. al. (1987), which has a comprehensive listing of events or behaviors. This served as a form of "open coding" in which all as much of the textual data as possible was assigned to some category. In the next stage a form of selective coding was n which a number of categories were developed the research questions, and others created based on ena seen in the texts, which reflected the language king of the respondents ("in vivo" or "emic"). The re then selectively analyzed according to these es. Davidman (1991) used as similar process:

nalyzed these transcripts and field notes by king for common themes, use of language, signs of affect, inconsistencies, repetition, key characters, dynamics, and connections between events (p. 71).

These more salient categories, or themes and patterns, become the conceptual material used to move toward theoretical integration.

While normally *grounded theory* would move toward developing analytical frameworks with relevance outside the research setting (the generic, statistical approach), I extended the analysis to the *macro foundations* within the *micro-order* following the principle of the *extended case method.* A criticism often leveled at ethnographic research is that micro-level analysis is too local and ahistorical, and while it may describe interesting cases, they are impossible to generalize to the population beyond that particular, unique case. In an attempt to get around this problem, Strauss employed *grounded theory* as a method of analysis and comparison across social contexts, enabling a construction of more generalizable social laws. While I used grounded theory to some extent as a technique of organization, I also applied the "extended case method" (Buroway 1991) in order to historically and socially situate what is going on at the micro level of congregations, school, and family. Buroway argues that grounded theory tries to tell us what how significant a case is in a statistical sense, that is, the likelihood that they will have similar attributes across social situations. The extended case method on the other hand is "genetic" rather than "generic" in that it

> ...tells us about the world in which it is embedded. What must be true about the social context or historical past for our case to have assumed the character we observed? Here significance refers to societal significance. The importance in a single case lies in what it tells us about society as a whole rather than about the population of similar cases (p. 281).

Another difference is in how grounded theory looks at natural settings as places where laws of human nature become visible. The extended case method looks at how the setting (for example rural Midwestern towns) is "a constellation of institutions located in time and space that shape domination and resistance" (p. 281).

In utilizing the extended case method I did not preclude other ways of looking at the micro order used by ethnographers and symbolic interactionists; these have proved invaluable over and over again, especially in studying religious subculture (e.g. Neitz 1990). A commitment to the extended case method simply means looking for the "macro foundations" within the "micro-order":

> In constituting the social situation as unique, the extended case method pays attention to its complexity, its depth, its thickness...works with given general concepts and laws about states, economics, legal orders, and the like to understand how those micro situations are shaped by wider structures (p. 281-282).

The *extended case method*, therefore, proved to be a useful framework as I began to link my findings to a theoretical framework that addressed the macro-structure *within* the micro-world.

Notes

[1]Those who were either born in the United States or lived most of their lives there, and who had at least one parent born in Mexico.

[2]As understood in its most basic sense as describing a culture (Spradley and McCurdy 1972), but also seeing culture in historical process (Willis 1981; Clifford and Marcus 1986), and as a set of skills or "cultural competencies" (Swidler 1986).

[3]The data gathered for this research was done primarily under the auspices of the Julian Samora Research Institute, which received approval from the (Michigan State) University Committee on Research Involving Human Subjects (UCRIHS) in August 1999 (Jorge Chapa and Ann Millard, Principle Investigators). In addition, the author received further approval to collect more data relative to religious questions (approved May 12, 2000; Steven J. Gold, Co-investigator).

[4]These guidelines are based on the New Ethnic and Immigrant Congregations Project (Warner and Wittner 1998: 8-10).

CHAPTER 4

The Community Context

The emergence of Latino faith communities is not happening in a social or demographic vacuum, but is tied to broader societal and regional changes, which have led to an increase in the settled Latino population, and a significant increase in the ethnic diversity of the Midwest. The purpose of this chapter is to look at what socio-demographic contexts are causing and shaping the emergence of Latino religious congregations in certain rural communities in Michigan and Indiana at *this particular time in history.*

CIDERVILLE AND BERRYVILLE[1]

The two Michigan communities in this study, Ciderville and Berryville, are located in Berry County in southwest Michigan. They are both easily accessible from an interstate highway, and a major rail line connecting Chicago with Detroit runs through both. Each town's main street is lined with red brick storefronts as well as quaint single-family houses. Each has its litany of traditional rural markers: water towers, taverns, small shops, fire stations, community libraries, and the K-12 public school. Many small, independent, Pentecostal and sectarian churches dot the landscape. A sign is posted on the road: "Repent and be baptized" just in front of *Leland's Well Drilling*. One observer noted quite accurately that "virtually all of the small towns in the area have a special 1950s look to them, as do the winding roads, and the roadside cafes--the look of vintage movies--and a firmly entrenched ethic of hard work, well-tended farms, and immaculate yards" (Griffith and Kissam 1995: 123). High School sports are popular, high profile events. Berryville High is a tough contender in football, as attested by its recent district championship.

The population of the two villages during the late 1990s was 3535.[2] The area did see some population growth during the 1980s of about 20 percent (while the state as a whole declined), and in the 1990s growth of 8.6 percent. The median income is $32,879 for Ciderville, and $29,583 for Berryville. Thirty-eight percent of the over-25 population in Ciderville has a high school education. Ten percent had a two-year college degree or higher. School officials reported that a high number of students (one third to half) moved to other parts of the county during the year. Ciderville's students nevertheless scored higher than expected on standardized tests.[3] Most of Berrryville High's seniors said they were headed for a two or four year college.

The dominant occupations are farming and related industries (packing, processing, greenhouses). On the road between the two towns there are a dozen or so major fruit packinghouses, processing operations, and small manufacturing plants. In Berryville a new industrial park has attracted a plastics manufacturer. All of these companies employ Latinos on both a seasonal and year round basis. A large greenhouse operation is located about halfway between the towns that employs about 30 Latinos permanently and up to 100 or more during the peak growing season. It is frequently cited as a major factor in Latino settlement in the area.

As you gaze up at the silver water tower that every small town in this state contains, a picture unfolds that reveals a new reality—in the foreground is *La Casa de Martinez* clothing store with a mural depicting scenes of Mexican-American life. Several other Mexican shops are also in view. To be sure, the presence of Latino families in this region is nothing new (I have met individuals whose families decided to settle here thirty years ago):

> If you visit [Ciderville] in the summertime and walk down Main Street or drop into a tavern, you are almost sure to see a number of Mexicans. They are the itinerant workers who come to harvest the fruit grown in the orchards in the area... (Dunbar 1968: 34-35).

These are the words of a historian comparing the region in 1968 with the 1920s. Were Dunbar writing that same passage today, and if he were an astute observer, he would have noticed the large public gatherings of *Mexicans* at the many churches, including the large and festive Mexican crowds at *St. Barbara's Catholic Church*, and the equally crowded halls of *Los Amigos Baptist Church* on any given Sunday (an increasing number of other congregations in the area have become either multicultural or entirely Latino). As well he would have noticed the increasing number of shops catering to the Latino market. These are all indicators that people of Mexican descent are no longer primarily "itinerant." Clearly a profound change has taken place since Dunbar wrote in 1968. What has indeed changed for this town is that it is undergoing part of the overall *browning* of the Midwest.

Migration

The fruit belt of southwest Michigan has long been a seasonal destination of farm workers. Its "lake effect" weather makes it ideal for various types of fruits and vegetables. Of the 44 labor intensive crops listed by the state, more than 30 are grown in this region. According to Valdes (1991) the seasonal migration to southwest Michigan from northeastern Mexico and southern Texas began in earnest in the 1960s. The earlier migrant workers were southern whites and African Americans. Growers also recall the migration of Caribbean workers from Jamaica and Haiti who worked the fruit and vegetables in the 1980s.[4] Today the migrant farmworkers presently are probably 98-99 percent Latino.

A research report published in 1994 by the Julian Samora Research Insititute (Aponte and Siles 1994) titled *Latinos in the Heartland: The Browning of the Midwest* argued that the overall population growth in the region is primarily due to the increase in the Latino population. In Michigan the number of Latinos increased 24% between 1980 and 1990, numbering 84,900 in 1990 (Aponte and Siles 1995). The native Latino presence is partly indicative of a long history of Mexican migration to the agricultural regions of Michigan.

Since the 1990s the Latino population has doubled in Ciderville. Ciderville had only 5.5 percent of its population listed as Latino ("Hispanic") in 1980, while in 2000 it is over 12 percent. The majority of growth in the 1980s of the Latino population in Michigan was not due to in-migration but to increases in the native population. Native Latinos contributed over 72% of the Latino population growth during the 1980s (Rosenbaum 1996). However it is unlikely that natural increase was responsible for the dramatic growth of Latinos in southwest Michigan during the 1990s. If the local Latino population base is large, the increase may be due to local Latino population growth. If the Latino population base is small, the growth is due to outsiders, from elsewhere in the U.S. or Mexico. Given that the Latino population base in the 1980s was not large, and that in the 1990s there has been a large increase in the Latino population, it is likely that the greater proportion of Latino population growth in Southwest Michigan is due to immigration, either directly from Mexico or via the border states.[5]

This conclusion is supported by observations of people working in local social service and educational institutions and attending Latino churches who observe that the settling population in the 1990s has percentages of Mexican nationals (*Mexicanos*) higher than in earlier decades. This not only increases the diversity of the Latino population, but tilts its interests toward the newly arriving population. This tendency is borne out in the ethnographic narratives and community profiles below, which detail masses celebrating *Nuestra Señora de Guadalupe*, clothing stores that specialize in apparel for *quinceañeras* (special recognition for 15-year old girls), and clubs that feature *Norteño* bands (for further analysis on this point Millard and Chapa, forthcoming).

Whatever their origin, there is clearly a growing population of settled Latinos even as the number of migrant workers has decreased. The likelihood of a more permanent Latino population is suggested in a study by

Rochin and Siles (1994) which shows that while the overall number of migrant[6] and seasonal workers in southwest Michigan has decreased from 1982 to 1992, the number of year round Latino agricultural workers has increased.[7] This increase has been sustained even in while the number of farms in the county decreased by 26 percent over the same time period.   In addition a substantial number of the Latino families who migrate may still be based in the Midwest. Twenty-two percent of migrant farmworkers in a study on pesticide knowledge listed Michigan as home (22 percent); most had worked on Michigan farms for over five years (Millard 1998).   When asked to list all the states where they had ever worked, 38 percent listed Michigan only.

The Mexican population in these communities is mostly dispersed throughout both the residential village and farming areas. There are several neighborhoods that have higher concentrations than others (including two trailer courts).   Several dozen families live near farms and greenhouses that hire large numbers of year round workers.

Intertwining Destinies

Moving out into the townships one does not have to travel far before the family farms begin. "The is the core of American agriculture: on one hand, seemingly unchanged since World War II; on the other, accepting the inevitability of a variety of social and economic changes" (Griffith and Kissam 1995: 123).   Some of these changes have meant a tough life for many rural families. Some growers have ceased operations due to retirement, or the children have not carried on the business.   Financially it has been difficult for some farms to continue. Prices for many fruit crops (tart cherries, apples, peaches) have remained flat. Recent imports of Chinese apple concentrate have depressed the market price to unprecedented levels. Many apple growers in 1999 had to dump their processing apples, unable to find buyers. Now the picture has been further complicated by a growing difficulty in guaranteeing an adequate supply of farm workers.

Ciderville has witnessed a significant "intertwining" of destinies between small farmers and migrant families for several decades. Some of these relationships have been positive, as evident in Rothenberg's (1998) interview with Karen Dawson. In the 1960s the Dawsons had as many as two hundred workers, half southern whites, half Latinos who lived in the labor camp. To deal with changing regulations they mechanized, and for the last twelve years the Dawsons have been working with one family, the Avilas. The Dawsons have learned to respect the cultural values of the Avilas, and see them very much similar to their own:

The Avilas have rural values. That's not typical of American culture. Rural values means that you're concerned with the well-being of your family above anything else. Rural values has your elderly mother here in your house with you. It doesn't have her somewhere else. The Avilas' main concern is their family, and it shows in their children...Quite frankly, I don't know what we'd do without the Avilas. They know how we do things and we know how they do things. Basically, the Avilas work our pickles. We wouldn't even put pickles in the ground if the Avilas weren't here. We split the pickle contract right down the middle with them.

The Dawsons feel a sense of pride in their work,
even the manual physical labor that is part of
farming (p. 65).

A similar case is the Dresdens. The Dresden family
farmhouse has the plaque out front which identifies it as a
"Centennial Farm," owned by the same family for over one
hundred years. They have farmed their land since 1861.
They grow a variety of fruits and vegetables, such as
apples, cherries, and asparagus. In 1969 they began hiring
Latino farmworkers. Previous to that it was southern
whites from Arkansas, Alabama, and Tennessee. To ensure
a steady supply of workers they would make occasional
trips to south Texas and make contact with crew leaders.
One person who came to work with the crew leader was
Felipe Cervantes. That began a relationship with the
Dresdens that has endured to this point, in a much more
permanent way than the Avilas.

Felipe and his sons eventually became tired of having
to move around wherever the crew leader placed them, and
they sought a more stable situation. They contacted Carl
about the possibility of wintering over with the Dresdens.
The Dresdens agreed and began considering the advantages
of having workers stay year round. They believed it would
lead to greater productivity and efficiency: workers would
not have to be trained in they way of doing things, it would
guarantee a stable work force, and they had enough to do in
the winter months to keep workers occupied. So they
encouraged Felipe and his sons to stay permanently with
them, with the option to return to Texas if they preferred.

From the mid-1980s Felipe and several of his sons
began to live year round in housing provided by the
Dresdens. They found the working conditions good; their

relationship with the Dresdens was characterized by mutual respect. Eventually they were able to purchase homes of their own. Most of Felipe's sons have become established in Michigan, working as foremen for the Dresden's.

Seasonal farmworkers like the Avilas, or permanent workers like the Cervantes, have been an essential feature of horticulture in this region. Carl says that when Latino farmworkers appeared on the scene in the late sixties it was a positive development for them. They proved to be industrious and hard working. "Life would be difficult without them," he admits.[8] Growers like the Dresdens with large enough operations to maintain a permanent workforce believe they are better off than those who must recruit new or returning workers each season.

Relationships between Growers and farmworkers like the Dawsons and Dresdens have been characterized by values of integrity, hard work, fairness and compassion. This has not always been the case. Just south of the Ciderville village is Hassle's labor camp notorious for being one of the worst in existence.

The intertwining of destinies is now coming full circle. Latinos are taking their place in these communities alongside farmers whose families have lived here for over a hundred years. Not only are Latinos buying rural homesteads, but they represent a growing proportion of the farmers in southwest Michigan.

En Michigan - A brief historical sketch[9]

Stayed here at the age of seven
Never went back to my Texas heaven
Didn't know why we had to stay
Why we had to work and play...*En Michigan*[10]

Federico first came to southwest Michigan with his family in 1954. His parents came to the United States in 1943 through the Bracero program. Federico was born in this country in 1950, and in 1955 his parents became registered aliens since they had a U.S.-born child. They would come up to Michigan with a *troquero*--a labor contractor who transported whole families and their belongings in a rig. In Michigan they would live in a grower's labor camp and work for different farmers within driving distance.

A young boy at that time, he recalls what is was like growing up in the migrant camps:

> One of the earliest pictures in my mind is 1957 in Fennville, but I have pictures in my mind from where we lived in Texas...in Michigan we were living at the farmer's barn. About ten paces from the barn was a trailer and my mom would go up the steps to use the kitchen...we moved three or four more times during the course of the year; and though we were residents we were still migrating, going back and forth to Texas.

In 1959 Federico's family pulled enough cash together and bought a farm in Fennville. Now they grew and picked their own pickles, beans, potatoes, and cauliflower. Federico's father liked Fennville. One of the *tiendas* reminded him of his hometown. Federico's older brother preferred Chicago, but their father was a *campesino* (a person who makes his living in farming), and that was the life he knew. Their father kept on doing this kind of work till he was 75 years old.

While many look at migrant farmworkers as lower status, needy and indigent, Federico always remembers his own experience with pride. His family had aspirations and began to realize them. First they decided to work their own farm instead of someone else's. Eventually they did move out from agriculture into other jobs. There was always a feeling of momentum

As many farm households needed additional income to survive, so in addition to their own farmwork, they kept working for other farmers, migrating down into the Ciderville area. Federico remembers working late into the night, and going to school during the day. He remembers his brother working at the aluminum processing plant in South Haven. He had to join the union, and he learned the language of unions—he'd come home and say phrases like "ratify the contract." "He worked so hard that he surpassed what they were supposed to make for piece rate, and he was told to "slow down."

Lucia, now a data entry clerk, first came to Michigan more than 20 years after Federico and his family. She remembers living in migrant housing as a child. The worst was in Florida, where they shared a shack with particularly large spiders; they couldn't afford anything better. The second worst was the Escondido camp in Berry County. She recalls the crowded and dirty cabins with outhouses, where you could hear everything going on with the neighbors. But she also remembers a more comfortable mobile home at a farm to the north, where the older couple her parents worked for treated them with decency.

Lucia's father Carlos was born in *Nuevo Leon, Monterrey,* Mexico. He attended technical college in Monterrey, and planned to get a degree in engineering. During those years he lived in a *colonia* called *Anahuac,* near *Valle Hermoso*, but went north seasonally to pick cotton in the Rio Grande Valley. Lucia's mother was born in Brownsville on the border in Texas, and had a lot of family in *Matamoros*, Mexico. She finished the sixth grade and later worked as a salesperson in a department store. On one of his trips north, Carlos passed through Brownsville and saw Lucia working in the window display. He decided he had to talk to her. They were married four months later. Lucia was the last born, preceded by three sisters and one brother.

Then began the long road that finally led to settling down in Berryville. In the 1970s Lucia's family joined the migrant stream coming up from *El Valle*, to Ohio, near Toledo, to work in the tomatoes and at the Starcross canning plant. As jobs became scarce in Ohio, Lucia's father remembered Michigan where he had traveled as a 17-year-old, and they decided to try it. For several years they moved around the fruit belt of southwest Michigan working blueberries and apples. As usual they lived in farm labor housing, some good, some bad, and never any privacy.

Marta, whom Federico would later meet and marry, came with her family to Dowagiac to work the strawberries. Her family worked alongside African American and Anglo pickers. As farmworkers they would travel through the Midwest by car with all their belongings. Sometimes they were not well received by the concessionaires along the way.[11]

Marta's father eventually became a crew leader and *troquero*. He began driving a truck, bringing workers up with him. She didn't attend school while in Michigan, only when in Texas. They spent some time in Chicago (about a year) before moving back to Michigan.

After one year of college she dropped out on account of her sister's death, and spent time with her mother, who had been especially devastated by the tragedy. After getting a job in one of the agencies serving farmworkers, she met Federico at an agency coordination meeting.

Marta remembers how Federico looked back then, long hair in ponytail, headband. The struggles for social justice throughout the nation were still intense, and attempts to improve conditions for farmworker were often met with intense opposition in Southwest Michigan. One grower just south of Ciderville repeatedly vandalized cars of social service and legal agencies serving the workers in his camp. On a number of occasions he threatened them at gunpoint. In one intense encounter he physically assaulted and injured Mr. Folgueras, an outreach worker from United Migrants for Opportunity (UMOI), and charged him with illegal entry. While Hassle dropped the charges against Folgueras, several parties, including UMOI, brought a case against Hassle. In 1971 the Michigan Attorney General ruled that the trespass law could not bar individuals from visiting the premises where farmworkers lived (i.e. they had rights that any other tenant has.)

The radicalism of activists such as Federico and others was incubated in the struggles to improve the quality of life for farmworkers. Federico worked in an agency delivering health services to migrant farmworkers and he remained active in issues affecting Latinos: health, housing, and education.

Federico was not alone in this work, but was part of a generation of dedicated Latinos who had grown up as farmworkers and who knew both the challenges and rewards of that kind of life. A number of them, like Federico, turned their radicalism toward pragmatic initiatives to improve the health and housing conditions of farmworkers. A number of these individuals saw their work bear fruit in the form of enduring institutions for health and housing and education.

Other examples include a Latino educator who had moved to the region from Texas and developed a model bilingual and migrant education program that has succeeded in getting large numbers of Latino youth into college. Still another had a vision for farmworker healthcare that developed into a high quality network of clinics that made high-quality affordable health care available to all people, including farmworkers. In 1973 the organization it had a budget of about $270,000, now it has a budget of $10.3 million.

There were also disappointments. An effort to build a welcome center (a "port of entry" facility), for migrant farmworkers was proposed in 1976. Some farmers supported it, along with a lot of agency people, but "you should have seen the opposition during the meeting at Lake Michigan College," Federico recalls. Leading up to this was the increase in a number of provisions designed to improve public health and the safety of housing for farm laborers. These changes forced many growers to either make significant investments or get out of housing altogether. A group of concerned farmers and people like Federico, had formed an organization called Rural Initiatives in Shelter and Education (RISE). Off-farm, affordable apartments were one option being explored, leading to the Sunrise Apartments in Keeler just south of Ciderville, built by RISE in 1983. The project was highly successful, and it was thought that this could be replicated in Ciderville. This led to the proposal by RISE in 1992 to put up a similar set of units on land to be purchased from the diocese of Kalamazoo just adjacent to St. Barbara's Catholic church. It was eventually abandoned after meeting with intense community opposition from "right and left." A later effort was made to purchase 40 acres for the welcome center behind a gas station near the Interstate. It was opposed and the project once again was dropped. Later the land was developed as a golf course.

Eventually Federico and Marta started a family, and had four children. At home they reinforced cultural values that they felt were important. He told them that if they listened to "los Beatles" music that had to also listen to *Tejano* or *mariachi* music the other half of the time. If they wanted to listen to country music, they had to listen to *Tejano* music too. Sometimes they resisted with "but dad that stuff is from the old country," but he kept reminding them of where they came from. A big part of Federico's activism is conveyed through music. He plays in a *Tejano* band that does comedy and cultural sensitivity training, and at mass he helps to lead the musicians who accompany the choir.

Marta went on to work as an ESL aid in the adult education program, first in Ciderville, then in the neighboring town where they bought a house. They were active in the church, which they saw go through growing pains as it evolved into a more multicultural congregation, with Latino members becoming the majority (in terms of numbers). Marta became an active lay leader in the church and her brother the same for a Latino congregation to the north.

When Federico was attending elementary school in Fennville his family was one of seven or eight Latino families in the entire community, a small fraction of the population. Now it is almost half the population. The

Latino population throughout southwest Michigan is now highly visible and growing rapidly. It is also more diverse than people realize. Many of those settling in Ciderville have been in farm labor for generations, and while many trace their roots to farmworkers from the Rio Grande Valley or Mexico, they have been joined by a growing secondary stream of migration out of large urban centers to smaller towns.[12] A significant number have moved from the Latino neighborhoods of Chicago where they were born and raised. Some, like the Sanchez family, have moved from Chicago to take up farming and run a grocery store.

The post office mural painted by Carlos Fuentes in 1934 is an illustration that Latinos have been established in southwest Michigan for many decades. Some like Federico have lived here most or all of their lives. With much effort, and sometimes against intense opposition, they were able to successfully launch health and educational organizations in response to perceived needs. These institutions have been an attraction to those who passed through this area seasonally, and many claim the good educational and health care systems are reasons they settled here permanently.

While many long-term residents spent time in the fields with their parents, they now occupy professional, well-paying jobs in the human services or other professions. However many have continued in the agricultural sector as foremen, supervisors in packing-houses, and crew leaders. Some growers began hiring year round workers as far back as the 1970s, which meant that a third generation is now coming of age--born and raised in Michigan. For families of long-term residents, the migration of extended family over several generations, as well as the bringing up of several generations in Michigan, has resulted in the establishment of kinship groups in Michigan and the Midwest.

Latinos have not only come from points south, but from west and east as well. Many from Chicago and (some from New York) have come to the areas seeking a "quieter" rural environment, more time for family, and safer schools. Some arrived to take up farm work, others purchased farms, *tiendas* (shops) and restaurants.

Growing Diversity

There is evidence that in the 1990s the proportion of Latinos moving seasonally and permanently to Michigan directly from Mexico increased compared with Mexican-Americans from the Rio Grande Valley or Florida. Furthermore, more of those are coming from states to the south of the traditional sending regions of the north-central states of Mexico, further increasing the diversity within the Latino population.

This change has made the cultural identity of immigrant Latinos more salient. This is seen not only in schools and the work force, but in the style of music heard in shops and clubs, and the religious celebration of the Virgin of Guadalupe, further indicators of an ever-growing diversity of the Latino community in terms of socio-economic class, nationality, and cultural identity. These differences sometimes produce tensions, as during the migrant housing debate at St Barbara's. The involvement in activism also reveals a difference between newcomers and older residents. Many well–established Latinos such as Federico have engaged the dominant culture to demand that public institutions be responsive to the needs of *La Raza*. Newcomers, whose grasp on resources and livelihood is less tenuous do not take the same posture. Isaac's comments (see Chapter 5) are more typical of the newcomers: "at first we were quiet and kept to ourselves." However a strong sense of solidarity with newcomers pervades the attitudes of the older residents. They have not forgotten where they have come from.

MEYERTON, NORTH CENTRAL INDIANA

> Five out of the six longest highways in the U.S. run
> within 20 miles of Meyerton.
> -sign at museum

You can get a variety of first impressions about a place depending on how you arrive there. If you arrive in Meyerton from the west (on one of the "six longest highways in the U.S.") you first pass a large automotive parts plant on the left, and immediately on your right is a very run-down trailer park with large puddles in the dirt driveway. A twin-prop aircraft is parked at the end of the trailer park's dirt track, imparting the scene with a feeling of contradiction. That is only the beginning of a series of surprises to the visitor who has time.

Continuing into the main downtown area you are greeted by the familiar mixed with the unfamiliar. The red brick, two story buildings which line the street are typical, but about half of the first story businesses have signs in Spanish. Venturing a walk along the main street you will notice that large number of customers are of Mexican-origin. Wandering into the rear of El Paraiso Market you can sit at the old soda fountain style counter (reminiscent of Woolworths except *Norteño* is playing loudly and the cook is frying *lengua* [tongue] for a *torta* [Mexican hamburger]).

Walking out the back door into the parking lot where taxis leave each Saturday for *Aguascalientes* state in Mexico, it is a short distance to the town square park. If you sit there long enough you will observe at least one, probably several Amish buggies pull up. Families will unload, the man, white shirt and black trousers or overalls, will tie up the horse to the chain. The women in blue dresses and bonnets will fill a bucket with tap water from the back of the fire station. They will walk to the dentist, bank, or Dollar Store.

As you observe the various items for sale in the windows you will come to one sizeable shop full of exotic carvings. On closer inspection there are African carvings of human figures, some as tall as 8 feet; there are many baskets of dried palm, and several masks. The mask looks *Shona*, they could be from Zimbabwe and South Africa. There is no sign on the door or name. You sense there is an interesting story behind this.

Moving west from the downtown area you come to the public library. It is unlike any small town library you have ever seen. It was built by money from Carnegie Foundation, in a neo-classical style of architecture with Greco-Roman columns. Going south you pass magnificent Victorian-style homes, some well preserved. One enormous pink house is now a bed and breakfast inn. The dining room ceilings were painted in Europe and brought here complete. Sliding doors have Honduran Mahogany on one side, Oak on the other (to match the other wood in the respective rooms). Across the street is a turreted house that has an elevator. Meyerton has seen splendorous times.

Farther up the street is a museum that was once a Jewish synagogue. Built in 1889 to serve the 60 Jewish families in town, the stain glass windows are still

magnificent.   There you will also learn that Meyerton was
founded by a man who happened to come from Meyerton
Pennsylvania.   In 1835 he "platted" the town Meyerton.
Meyerton Pennsylvania continues to be a sister city, and
one of the mayoral responsibilities is to attend the sister
town's parades. (One year the mayor drove Meyerton's fire
truck Indiana to the parade in Pennsylvania.)

These days tourism is down.   The Marshmallow
Festival used to attract more interest, but since the
Marshmallow Factory closed down the town can no longer
make the claim of being one of the largest producers of
Marshmallows in the world.   The economic base
fortunately does not rely on tourism.   The town has always
had an industrial base.   The museum has samples of the
cold boxes (what modern people call refrigerators), and
photographs of the buggies made locally. Industry now
attracts people from both near and far.   A large industrial
park employs around 3500 workers (only about 4000
people live in Meyerton).   Products vary from exhaust
systems to plastic bottles.

While at the museum you can enlist the willingness of
several volunteers from the Historical Society to share
some anecdotes about Meyerton's rather unusual past.
Meyerton is unique among small Midwestern towns for it
has a precedent of being home to a large immigrant
community, more like Chicago than *Middletown*. (The
town seal has the Star of David among its other images).
Looking back over Meyerton's ethnic history puts the
current process of "mexicanization" in better perspective,
for it has been a community constantly recreated by
"outsiders"—first by Jewish refugees, next by "hillbillies"
from Appalachia, and most recently by Latinos of Mexican

descent. Its ethnic history has also been characterized by an attitude of exclusion toward outsiders.

The Jewish Era[13]

Meyerton's Jewish phase began in the 1850s with the arrival of Jewish refugees fleeing persecution in Prussia. Two Jewish peddlers, Frederick Rosenburg and Solomon Hillel found the town attractive, partly due to the atmosphere of religious tolerance among the German Mennonites and Amish who had also began settling Wayne County (Chamber of Commerce). It is said they were also aware of plans to put a rail line through the town, saw potential business opportunities, and decided to settle permanently. Their small-scale retail business was prosperous. Later they became business rivals as they expanded their economic ventures into banking, manufacturing (buggies, cold boxes) a network of electric railways, and the largest real estate agency in the United States. The descendants of these men continued the economic empires begun by Rosenburg and Hillel.

According to most town historians and old timers, this era of the town's history (from the late 1800s to the late 1920s) was the town's "golden age." In the words of one town historian it was a booming "Jew town," "in it's youth", "coming up," rapidly expanding, with beautiful streets, three banks, and a booming economy. The temple *Ahavas* was built in 1889. Many expansive Victorian mansions were built, planned by architects from as far as Chicago. Many of these mansions are still on mainstreet. The temple, with its magnificent stained glass windows, would later become the historical museum.

A favorite pastime of locals during this era of affluence was to go to the train station and watch wealthy families return from Chicago decked out in their latest acquisitions. The wealth was also displayed during the high holidays:

> Everybody in Meyerton dressed very elegant and were very somber and sedate during New Year's [Rosh Hashanah] services. And everybody always wore hats, and also gloves for the women—you didn't go to temple without them.[14]

The Amish farmers of the surrounding farms also had descended from Anabaptists fleeing religious persecution in Europe. The Amish would come into town to do business on Saturdays. The Jewish merchants allegedly convinced the rabbi to allow them to go to temple on Sunday instead of Saturday so they could do business with the Amish farmers.

One of the town historians I spoke with had worked as a maid for the Hillel family in the 1920s. In her view the Jewish community during this golden age clearly occupied the upper strata of that society, revealing the class divides of that era. One of her duties was to help cater dinner parties, and she spoke of these lavish affairs in a way that revealed something of the elegance of their lifestyles. During one party she was told to use the "silver pitcher." Not knowing the difference between silver and aluminum she used the aluminum and was reprimanded for this serious breach of propriety.

In 1919 the Rosenberg State Bank was called Meyerton's Rock of Gibraltar, by far the largest in the locality its total resources were $1,005,486.61. The depression of the 1930s ended the "golden age" as well as the rivalry between the Hillel and Rosenberg families. Faced with the possibility of bankruptcy of both family-owned banks, they pooled their resources and merged into a single bank.

At the height of the Jewish era, (circa 1890), about sixty families lived in Meyerton. By the 1920s their number had dwindled to 24 families. Families with the wherewithal to educate their children did so, and the youth saw no future in a town of under 2,000. After World War II Meyerton's Jewish era was clearly over. In 1981 the last Jewish individual in Meyerton died. Many of these individuals were buried in the Jewish section of the Meyerton cemetery, with Hebrew inscriptions on the stones.

By this time had seen the town had seen the presence of highly visible groups from outside the Anglo-American mainstream of America—Jews from Prussia and Mennonites from Germany. Now as the Jewish population aged and dwindled, several other waves of newcomers would soon change the town's character.

The Hillbillies

In the 1950s there began a great migration of people out of the economically depressed coal mining regions of Appalachia. Coming from states like Kentucky, West Virginia, and Tennessee they migrated north to the industrial cities. Over a period spanning about 20 years some of these so-called "hillbillies" found their way to Meyerton.

Very little has been written about these people, their sense of communal identity, and what kind of reception they found in Meyerton. Though not racially different from the original inhabitants of the town, they came to occupy a different subculture and socioeconomic class. Their influx reportedly caused a serious housing shortage. Those who remember claim that the town saw them as outsiders, poor, uneducated, and generally undesirable element.

The "Browning" of Meyerton

"With a population of about 4,000, Meyerton in Wayne County appears to be one of the cities or towns in northeast Indiana most affected by the growth of the Hispanic population," observed the regional press. [15] Meyerton is one of the Midwestern towns that have truly experienced what Aponte and Siles (1995) predicted about where immigration would have one of its most dramatic impacts in the future—not in the expected urban points of entry such as Miami, New York, or Los Angeles—but in small towns of the Midwest.

Latino Pioneers

In the 1960s another group had begun to make its appearance, albeit seasonally. Migrant farmworkers from Texas came in great numbers to work in the region's tomato farms. There used to be a big labor camp in to the west in Plymouth. Andy Flores and his family were the first Mexican-Americans to settle in Meyerton. He arrived in 1960 he says, with "75 cents in my pocket, my wife and two kids." He was the first Mexican to work in the Plax factory (which later became Botex). He said he "felt welcomed in Meyerton with open arms," and soon bought a house. At that time factories were recruiting southern labor (hillbillies), but they couldn't find enough workers for the difficult swing shifts, and they kept advertising for more workers. In the 1970s four farmworker families decided to settle permanently in Meyerton. They also worked for industries such as Botex.

New Immigrants

The trickle of families who joined the pioneers became a wave in the late 1980s and early 1990s. By the early 1990s the people of Mexican descent really began to make their presence felt. The economic context in a nutshell is that during the early 1990s north central Indiana (Elkhart, South Bend, Fort Wayne), which earlier had been hit hard by the deindustrialization of the American economy, began to ride the present economic boom and reemerge with a dynamic manufacturing base.[16] Smaller communities like Meyerton attracted auto component companies who relocated out of Detroit to out-maneuver unions and take advantage of other lower production costs. By 1990 the growth in employment due to manufacturing had already increased 270 percent.[17] Soon the demand for production workers outstripped the local supply. Turnover was high, especially in the more demanding second and third shifts.

Mexican workers from the pioneer families had by this time already proved themselves as model workers. Some of these long-term employees were asked by companies to recruit additional workers, and they did, bringing friends and relatives from Mexico, the border region, and other parts of the United States. These types of jobs were attractive in that they generally paid much better than field labor, and had more favorable working conditions such as bathrooms, paid leave, year-round employment (see Martin et. al. 1996).

In the early 1990s larger numbers of workers of Mexican descent came up to the industrial parks of north central Indiana, and many eventually found their way to Meyerton. Although the in-migration of Latinos began to pick up in the 1980s, it was from 1993-on that many residents remember as the period in which large numbers of Latinos were noticed moving into Meyerton. For example, it was in the early 1990s that school officials began to report much larger numbers of "Spanish language minority" students (15 percent in 1994).[18]

The economic stagnation of the Mexican economy plus the family sponsorship of those who became residents under the IRCA (Immigration Control and Reform Act) provision added momentum to the social networks linking Meyerton with states in Mexico. Several of those interviewed in the Latino community identified IRCA as a kind of catalyst for new migration to the region. In addition, lower cost of living, and less competition from other Mexican American and Mexican-born workers gave this area certain advantages over the Southwest (Binational Study 1997).

Latino Community Profile

In 1995 the mayor commissioned an unofficial count, which utilized bilingual, mostly Latino volunteers. The survey numbered 731 " Hispanic" living in Meyerton, and 803 if a trailer court just south was counted. However those taking the survey believed it highly likely that this was an undercount, and estimated that the actual number could be as high as 1200. One indicator of this is was that school enrollment data showed over a hundred more children than were counted in the survey. This higher estimate of 1200 even surprised some in the Latino community who expected the number to be around 900.[19] If the unofficial count in 1995 was fairly accurate, it means that even the Census Bureau estimates for 1998 (1014 Hispanics for the entire county) were probably too low.[20]

The most recent census figures[21] show a total of 1,451 (all but five of whom were of Mexican descent). Given that the official number is probably an undercount, the growth in the Latino population has been truly dramatic, from around 300 at the beginning of the decade (8.5 percent of the population, to 1451 (or 33.5 percent of Meyerton's population) at the decade's end. It shows two important changes that were already assumed, that 1) Meyerton's population is one-third Latino, and 2) that Meyerton's population increase from 3443 to 4357 or 914 persons is entirely due to in-migration of Latinos. During the decade Meyerton's white population actually declined from 3301 to 3191, or three percent, while Meyerton's Latino population increased from 321 to 1451, or 352 percent.

The 1995 survey identified some characteristics of the burgeoning Latino population:

70 percent of adults were employed;
85 percent considered themselves permanent residents of Meyerton;
95 percent were interested in becoming American citizens;

Pastor Cervantes, an unofficial spokesman for the Latino community believed that of those surveyed, 98 percent were of Mexican descent, and 25 percent were born in the U.S., many of whom had lived previously in Texas,

Florida, or California. He also believed that many who had planned to return to Mexico or the southern U.S. now wanted to stay in the area; and ninety-nine percent want to learn English. Those who know the Mexican population believe that most of those who immigrated from Mexico come from the Mexican state of *Aguascalientes*. These families reportedly maintain frequent contact with relatives and friends in *Aguascalientes*.[22]

Interviews with youth and adults who moved to Meyerton in the 1990s suggest that the major attraction was industrial jobs, and in the case of workers from Mexico it was the wage differential between the United States and Mexico. Those who arrived in the early 1990s have been followed by family members. High school students who were interviewed all had relatives here before they arrived.

The Mexican presence is highly visible in the old downtown area. The downtown has the typical red brick two-story buildings, but many businesses are oriented to the Mexican market. A large *tienda* (whose owner was born in *Durango* State of Mexico, but has lived many years in Chicago) has a full line of produce, as well as *taqueria* (taco stand) and *carniceria* (butcher). In addition there are the restaurants, clothing stores, *Officina de Servicios* (services like notary public, money transfer--*Western Union, Cart Mex, Uniteller*), *Servicio de Impuestos*, video libraries, a floral and bridal shop with sign saying "se habla espanol," Billiards, with a sign "Billar", and the landmark *Eli's Tacos*. *Lake Bank*, the descendant of the *Meyer and Hillel Bank*, has a large Mexican clientele.

The second stories of the buildings lining the main street have largely been converted into weekly rentals which house primarily newly arrived Mexican tenants. Other newcomers live in three very run-down trailer parks outside of city limits, one to the south. Some of the more upwardly mobile are buying and building houses in better, residential parts of the city. The long-time Latino residents have lived in these better parts of town for several decades.

The Latino community in Meyerton is made up essentially of two sub-groups. The first is the *pioneers* and their children and grandchildren. Theirs is a community bound together by *kinship*--many have common grandparents, *class*--they are middle class professionals, teachers, policemen, business owners, and *religion*--most belong to Templo Rey or one of the other Pentecostal churches.) Many of the businesses they operate (shops, translation services, real estate) have been created to serve the new immigrant population. The second subgroup is rapidly growing *newcomers*, those who have moved from the border states and Mexico to the town in the 1990s. They are largely unskilled production or service workers, monolingual Spanish speakers, mostly Roman Catholic churches, who occupy the crowded apartments downtown or in one of the trailer parks.

Community Comparisons

Ciderville and Meyerton represent two very different social contexts of Latino settlement and community formation. In Ciderville (and Berryville) the growth of the Latino population has been gradual, accelerating somewhat in the last decade. The population is very rural and dispersed, economically engaged in agro-industry or human service professions serving migrant farmworkers. Meyerton, although essentially rural, has a large industrial base which has attracted a significant in-migration of Mexican nationals in the 1990s which transformed the town's population. Racial polarization in Meyerton was openly articulated, particularly during the time when new immigrants asserted themselves in public space, (e.g. downtown.)

In both communities, migration will likely continue to be a function of the expanding social pathways that "energize" wage differentials and perpetuate continued immigration to particular destinations (Massey 1994). Within this context of migration, settlement, and ethnic assertion, Latino religious congregations will continue to play critical roles in communal life.

Notes

[1] All names of places and people fictitious.

[2] The population and income data in this section are from the 1990 and 2000 census, retrieved from the U.S. Census Bureau website, factfinder.census.gov, May 20, 2003. It does not include data from the surrounding townships.

[3] Detroit Free Press, 1/20/98.

[4] The Grand Rapids Press, 11/18/1980.

[5] Rene Resenbaum of JSRI, personal correspondence. According to Rosenbaum, whether the growth is due to locals, out of state residents, or immigrants depends on the specifics of each local area, particularly the size of the Latino population base

[6] Data for migrant farmworkers is estimated. A "migratory agricultural workers" is defined by the State of Michigan as "an individual whose principal employment is in agriculture on a seasonal basis, who has been employed within the past twenty-four months, and who establishes for the purpose of such employment, a temporary residence" (Rochin and Siles 1994: 4).

[7] "Seasonal agricultural workers" are those working less than 150 days of the year, and a "regular hired worker" has worked more that 150 days in the state, and whose principal employment is in agriculture (Rochin and Siles 1994).

[8] Interview with Carl Dresden, 11/15/99.

[9] Guillermo Martinez, a poet, musician, employment specialist, and advocate for Latino causes provided personal insight and a much

needed "insider's" perspective to this narrative. He also wrote the lyrics of *En Michigan,* which portrays with poetic force the experience of one Latino family. The following historical narrative uses personal histories as backdrops to illustrate the patterns of migration, settlement, and struggle of Latinos in southwest Michigan.

[10]From the song/poem En Michigan, copyright 2001 LuaLyric Pub. Co/Transom Music Co. From the CD La Onda Del Midwest/Los Bandits. Words: Guillermo Martinez. Music: Rene Meave. All rights reserved.

[11]Another family remembered similar experiences: "In Arkansas when they ran out of gas he [father] sold his shotgun to fill the tank...in Missouri when they ran out of gas he sold another spare tire. 'It was my Dad's faith and will that brought our family to Michigan,'" said his son (Kalamazoo Gazette, 8/7/99).

[12]During fieldwork in Grand Rapids I came to know a sizeable Cuban and Dominican population who had come from New Jersey and New York.

[13]Information about the Jewish colony is from Chamber of Commerce documents and interviews with members of the Meyerton Historical Society.

[14]AL 11/16/95; AL is an abbreviation for the local trade paper. The actual name is not used in order to protect the anonymity of respondents.

[15]AL 3/5/00.

[16]Historically the Midwest has had more industrial job opportunities than the Southwest, and one-third of all industrial jobs in the U.S. between 1950 and 1970 were found there (Saenz and Cready 1996).

[17]Community Patterns and Trends Summary, The Indiana Total Quality of Life Initiative, 1994.

[18]AL 11/17/94.

[19]AL 3/23/95.

[20]AL 3/5/00.

[21]U.S. Census Bureau website (census.gov) DP-1 Profile of General Demographic Characterisics: 2000, for [Meyerton], IN.

[22]Small numbers of other Latino nationalities have historically lived in Meyerton, for example Puerto Ricans. Factories in Meyerton reportedly employ workers from Central and South America. However the local school attendance clerk (a Mexican American) knows of only Mexican-origin students.

Community of Memory:
St. Barbara's Catholic Church

Spanish-speaking Catholicism predates the Pilgrims and existed in parts of the United States annexed for statehood (the Southwest and California). The Catholic Church in the U.S. is estimated to be about 35 percent Latino (Hernández 1996), and 57 percent of Latinos identify themselves as Catholic (Keysar, Kosmin and Mayer 2002).[1] Latino Catholicism[2] represents a unique religious identity developed in the United States by people of Latin American descent. The emergence of a Latino Catholicism began with the urban migration in post-WWII American and grew out of the more militant Latino/Chicano social movements in the late 1960s and early 1970s. (The history of this development is already well documented; see Ana Marie Diaz-Stevens 1994, 1998; Anthony M. Stevens-Arroyo 1994, 1998). Stevens-Arroyo (1994) describes how a Latino group identity "crystallized" around the following characteristics which define Latino Catholicism today: language, religious faith, shared traditions, values, symbols, literature, folklore and music, and certain political issues.

The ideology of change and anti-colonialism that spilled over into the church fostered an important shift:

This new identity differed from the Latino image of the 1950s and early 1960s. No longer was the

burden of change and adaptation lay exclusively on
Latinos seeking to be Americanized: now, America
itself was expected to change. Most importantly,
the process of change required native Latinos to
assume leadership for their own people (p. 110).

Since those years Latino Catholics generated major
institutional changes, especially in dioceses where they
were powerful such as New York, Los Angeles, and New
Mexico (Diaz-Stevens 1994). Institutional struggles were
waged for more representation; masses and music were
developed by Latinos that reflected and incorporated
various Latin cultures (such as the *Misa Jibara* and the
Easter or *Triduum* processions). In sum, Latino
Catholicism experienced a resurgence that unmistakably
affirmed its unique character (Stevens-Arroyo 1998).

As radicalism waned a fragmentation among various
ethnic and ecclesiastical groups reemerged (for example
around the movement of liberation theology), and Latino
Catholicism is still challenged by intra-ethnic differences.
In assessing the current state of Latino Catholicism,
Arroyo-Stevens believes that the institutional church is still
more comfortable with the image of Latinos as immigrants
rather than a "conquered" people, but who are actively
creating cultural space with the church. This reflects the
current neo-conservative climate in America, and
minimizes the need for special attention to Latinos
(Stevens-Arroyo 1994).

ST. BARBARA'S CATHOLIC CHURCH

St. Barbara's Catholic Church is a multicultural (but
primarily Latino) parish, with a history of "mission" work

to the newly arrived and migrant Latino population. Catholicism has a long history in southwest Michigan with the presence of French missionaries in the early 1700s. Indigenous to this region were the Potawatomi Indians, and many accepted the Catholic faith. One of the oldest Catholic churches in the region was built on land donated to the diocese by Chief Leopold Pokagon. Because they were openly practicing Catholicism the Pokagon band was able to negotiate its way out of being forcibly removed to Kansas.

St. Barbara's was founded as a parish in 1947.[3] In the 1960s Latinos began visiting mass. The Bishop made a decision in the 1970s that the Ciderville Parish would reach out to Latino Catholics living in the region, even those outside of the parish boundaries. Previously, priests and lay members would visit and hold mass in the labor camps (some still do), but the Bishop's decision was an invitation to be fully part of the parish, to come celebrate the mass in Spanish. This was implemented through the work of Father Bill who in 1989 became parish pastor and diocese coordinator for Latino ministry, and was part of the "Bishops Committee" for the Latino ministry. He had for many years ministered in nearby farm labor camps and was fluent in Spanish and familiar with the culture. As parish priest he worked to make the Latino group feel welcome, giving mass in Spanish, and involving them in programs to give them sense of ownership in what the church was doing. He also worked closely with the Anglo membership to move it toward becoming a "community of welcome."

The Latino membership began to grow rapidly through the "missionary" efforts of bilingual priests (including Vincentian priests, and several others from Colombia) directed mostly at newly settled and migrant families in labor camps. These and Father Bill's efforts quickly earned the trust of the people and community. The impact of these various individuals was that the church became a "community of welcome," and Latino membership exploded.

The congregation was ethnically mixed for a long time. Parishioners remember that many of the earliest members were European immigrants who spoke Polish, German, and Czech. As these groups assimilated it lost its immigrant identity. Latino members went to English mass, although "they rejoiced" whenever there was mass in Spanish. The significance (and insight) of the Bishop's decision to meet the needs of the newer Latino population was revealed in an observation by one long-time Latino member of the parish:

> Before the Bishop's decision there was a problem in seeing the Latino population as separate from the existing congregation, as indigent...people we send missionaries to. The problem of being the object of missionary activity is that it implied that those who are targeted are somehow deficient or helpless. This plays well in the media and in the public misperception that Latinos applied for residency under IRCA's amnesty provision because it entitled them to food stamps.

Father Bill was not comfortable either with the notion of "sending missionaries" to the Latinos around Ciderville, and believes "some damage was done." While he realizes that the Vincentian order is "missionary minded," that it is part of their spirit, he admits it did not facilitate their incorporation into parish life: "It was almost like they had to rent the church from us." He feels more should have been done to bring them into full participation, like serving on the parish council.

Becoming a multicultural parish has not been an easy task. One of the biggest tensions grew out of an effort by an agency to purchase some church property to build off-farm farmworker housing. The church held town meetings on the matter. Many community members opposed the project and attacked it. One parishioner remembered that during one really packed meeting Anglo residents made some "racist" remarks such as "its going to bring down the neighborhood... there will be junk around, and lowrider cars." She said, "You could see the lines drawn" with those supporting it mostly Latino (with some Anglo supporters), and a huge block of Anglos huddled on the other side (including some Latino families).

But many parishioners remember the issues were not that easily divided along racial and ethnic lines. The Latino membership was also split on the issue. Some Latinos, mostly those whose families have lived in the region for several generations, opposed the project on the grounds that the proximity to the church would place too many burdens on the priest. While they supported housing for farmworkers, they were uncertain that the agency implementing the project was truly competent and fair.

While many in the congregation supported the plan, a consensus emerged in the church community that it would not be a good idea. Two factors converged to veto the project, (1) backlash from the Anglo community at large, and (2) opposition of some church members who felt it was not good for the church. Father Bill could have proceeded with the plan since community approval was not required, but he and the council didn't want to be seen as doing something in opposition to the community. The ordeal left relationships between Anglo and Latino members strained.

What ensued after that was described by one former leader as a period of " turmoil." Father Bill took another post and a Spanish priest was brought in who did not help stabilize the situation or reduce tensions, but rather created a lot of dissension. Many felt he looked down on them as poor and uneducated; attendance dropped. The members appealed to have him removed. They even took it as far as the Mexican consulate in Detroit; such was the "depth of pain and hurt" that his actions caused. One issue that was clarified during this time was that "territorial rules" did not apply to Latino members. Those living outside the parish boundaries are welcomed. Eventually the priest was replaced. Father Bill returned as interim pastor.

The current priest, Father Rafael, is a South American who has lived in the U.S. for five years. He says mass in both Spanish and English. Since the word is getting out to more and more that the priest speaks Spanish, Father Rafael's life is becoming busier. People drop by unexpectedly to ask for help with all kinds of problems, and there are the customary weddings and funerals. He is getting his Masters degree in counseling psychology because he feels that many of the members, especially migrants, don't have good options for getting mental health services. He said he is in a good position to help them since they trust and confide in him.

The priest doesn't know the exact number of Latinos who attend, because some pass through and don't register. But those actually attending Spanish mass are about 400. In summer the priest must say mass twice on Sunday to the Spanish members to accommodate larger crowds. One member pointed out that "in the past, during the winter, you could put all the Hispanic members in the center section of the church. Now it is standing room only."

By virtue of its size and its ministries conducted both by and for Latinos, St. Barbara's is probably the most *significant* Latino organization in the region. The parish is clearly perceived and experienced as a community of welcome. A tangible sign of this was seen during the summer of 1999 when a new center was opened next to the rectory. It was named after a Mexican family whose father's generosity was so great it "exasperated his family and friends."[4] During the fruit season the center is stocked with good used clothing and household items.

Bridges

St. Barbara's is a multi-cultural and multi-lingual parish, with both English and Spanish-speaking congregations and some Potawatomi Indians. The Anglo membership numbers about 150, much smaller numerically but still influential in council decisions. The transition to becoming a predominantly Latino parish, as we have seen in the short history of the parish, not always been a smooth one. The current priest, Father Rafael, is trying to keep the faithful together through this phase of parish history. He is a bridge builder, striving to forge a united community out of the Anglo and Latino congregations. He sees the relationships between the two groups fortunately as positive, marked by a high degree of mutual respect. According to Joyce, a long-time lay leader of African-American and Native American heritage, Father Rafael "has been good at bridging the communities. When they come together for meetings and make a decision, he says 'the people of the church have said this.'" She believes the parish has been through the hardest transition:

> Fortunately now, we have been through turbulent and strong winds, we are now over the mountain in the foothills on the other side...they are growing together...the pain is a lot less...I feel there is a lot less bias than before...The majority are looking for ways to come together.

People like Jim are also helping bridge the cultural divide. I noticed Jim from the beginning since he was sometimes the only other Anglo at Spanish mass. Jim is a former seminarian who has worked with the priests who ministered in the labor camps. Being bilingual he attends both Spanish and English masses, and teaches a catechism class. Catechism classes are taught in English, but if some students need words translated he can help. On several occasions Jim has been asked to be sponsor for confirmation, a particularly Mexican practice, and according to Joe, an honor for him.

"To Be with my People"

As I became a sort of habitue at the parish, I began to run into certain people on a regular basis. One of those people was Fernando. I met him at the Concerned Latino Parents Group meeting. Several weeks later I met him after mass at a food sale to raise money for the celebration of Nuestra Senora de Guadalupe. At the next mass I attended I walked in late to see him and four others up front holding signs during the priests' homily (there were illustrating different styles of parenting). The next day we met on more common ground—McDonalds.

Fernando was born in *Queretaro* in 1962. He picked cotton at an early age, and when he was 14 came to Arizona to pick cotton or fruit. He and his older brothers were the pioneers—the first of their family to make the journey north. Crossing the desert into Arizona by foot, they eventually caught a ride with a Navaho man going to Phoenix. On the way to work in Florida they were picked up by the INS in New Mexico and deported.

The next year he went to Idaho to join an uncle working there. They worked in potatoes and grain. The following year he returned to Idaho. He intended to go from there to Florida. Meanwhile his uncle was in Bangor and then called to tell him there was work there. Fernando decided to follow his uncle's lead and stop in Michigan on his way to Florida. He came and worked the *Triple T* farm. Then, just before leaving for Florida they were picked up by INS agents and deported. This was fall of 1978.

The next year he returned to Michigan. While at Hardings he met his wife Celia (whom he had seen the previous year at St. Barbara's.) Her family had stopped migrating in 1974. Now with Fernando she rejoined the migrant stream between Michigan and Florida in 1979. In 1980 their first son was born in Florida, and in 1981 they were married. Not having cither much money or family around, he and his bride settled for a courthouse ceremony.

In 1984 they decided to stop migrating. They felt that migration was not the best situation for raising a family. Fernando had found year-round farm work with several growers in southwest Michigan. In 1986 his wife Celia landed a job recruiting for a migrant Headstart program. In 1988 they moved to a house in Bangor, the town where his wife's family was living.

In 1993 he worked as a bus driver for the same migrant Headstart that his wife worked for. In 1994 he began the job he holds at present, maintaining school buses and working as a substitute driver. He learned the skills he needed to do his present job from other work, such as the foreman job he held in South Haven, where he was responsible for fixing equipment. He learned English at an alternative school and later at an ESL program, but his English soon became too good to continue ESL classes. He kept working on his high school diploma at an alternative school until he graduated in 1998 (after 10 years of work).

Fernando and Celia, who now work at the local savings bank, have four children, all born in Michigan except the oldest son who was born in Florida. He is 19, works in Holland at a furniture plant, and did not finish high school. The oldest daughter is 15, a freshman at high school, and is an active member of the church youth group. She was also at the meeting where I first met her father. Another daughter is nine, and the youngest son is five.

While visiting Fernando and his family at their home, I was shown a photograph of Fernando's siblings (nine altogether) and parents. Most of them live permanently in the U.S. Since 1986, three of his brothers have moved to southwest Michigan, two live in his neighborhood. His father still comes from Mexico each year to work the fruit. He says it's good having so much family around; they stop by to see each other; if there is a problem or you need something, want to borrow a tool, or need someone to watch the kids, there is always help.

It is common around Ciderville to find family units like Fernando's who have followed in a chain after the "pioneers." His uncle built a network between communities that eventually led to four brothers settling in a particular town in Michigan (see Chapter 4). It is also important to recognize the role that the church community played in the formation of kinship units. Fernando first met his wife at the church. As one of the major gathering places for Latinos in the region, many families grew out of relationships started there.

I asked Fernando what his involvement with the parish meant to him and his family:

F: I go there for two reasons, it's in Spanish, and there I can be with my people. [I asked him what he meant by "my people," do you mean friends?]

F: No, to be with other Mexican people.

KC: Why do you require your children to go to church?

F: Mostly because it's in Spanish.

KC: Do you think it helps preserve the language?

F: Yes.

KC: Would you go if the mass were only in English?

F: Probably not.

KC: What if there were no Spanish mass, but a Protestant church held services in Spanish, would you go?

F: No.

KC: Do you ever attend the Friday night youth group that your daughter is part of?

F: I would but I work the late shift. It's good that they go... she likes the meetings, and parents are there as well because they want to know what the kids are doing.

I asked Fernando about his children's experience in this culture, if he thought his children were becoming too Americanized by growing up here:

> F: I don't think so; they speak only Spanish at home.
> KC: Will being Mexican hinder your children, keep them from getting ahead?
> F: No. I want them to be proud of their culture. Like at home they listen to mostly norteño, ranchero, and mariachi music. For me, the people I work with are very interested in my culture. Especially one of my teachers. They are also lay preachers at another [Protestant] church.

Fernando represents a substantial group within the parish of first generation Mexican Americans who have settled in one of the small towns within striking distance of St. Barbara Catholic Church. They have struggled to find decent jobs and homes, learn the English language, and to provide stability for their children, whom they are now raising in primarily Anglo communities. While Fernando and his family could attend a Catholic church within their town, they choose to drive the 20 miles to St. Barbara's.

The reasons he gives are to be with those with whom he shares a common culture, ("to be with my people"), and to expose his children to that culture ("because its in Spanish"). Fernando's rhetoric about language is a type of code that refers to something deeper –the affirmation of certain cultural traditions. For example, the Latino children at St. Barbara's can tell you who all their relatives and baptismal godparents are. I witnessed numerous events, (such as baptisms, blessings of automobiles) in which Latino or Mexican traditions were honored.[5]

Fernando's statements show the church is a community of memory not only for him but for his children as well. It was Fernando's primary reason for ensuring that his daughter attend church (rather than spiritual reasons, although those could have been taken for granted). The church as an important cultural resource for the second generation emerged as a dominant theme in interviews with parents, although it was not always articulated with such intentionality as in Fernando's case (the second generation had a different perspective on the matter as seen below). Sometimes parents would simply state a preference for the language, or talk about the congregation as a place to see friends and family.

Misa en español *(Spanish mass)*

Summer or winter, Spanish mass is always crowded. If you arrive you will find the parking lot overflowing with pickups, and vans, spilling out along the street. Inside it is standing room only, full of families and children, and large numbers of young, single men as well. Teenage males stand in the back, hanging out with friends; gold chains and crucifixes are *de riguer*. Most people are dressed in neat and clean street clothes, new jeans, cowboy boots, and shirts without neckties; older women are in dresses, younger women and girls dressed more casually.

The service is strongly flavored by music. Three or four guitarists, an accordionist, and a vocal group with a Mexican folk sound serenade the congregation. Carlos walks back and forth vigorously leading the enthusiastic congregational singing. When they begin serving the communion, the musical group leads singing about "*somos el cuerpo de Cristo*," and "*Cristo esta en nosotros*." There is a light, joyous atmosphere that the songs and musicians create as people line up to take the bread and wine.

The liturgy is found in the misalette, which contains the readings for that particular week in both Spanish and English. The misalette was originally written in Latin, and then translated into Spanish. The type of Spanish used in the translation however is not used in Mexico, which has its own translation. The large red book used by the priest at St. Barbara's is the Mexican version.

The use of traditional instruments and language combine to make St. Barbara's a culturally familiar place for Latinos of Mexican origin, a place where the "thin thread of memory" connects the past to the future. However the music and liturgy are by no means simply transplants from Mexico. The music is a style of "Mexican gospel" with a hint of *Tejano*, developed in the United States. Most of the songs come from a hymnal called *Flor y Canto*, developed by a catholic laywoman from New Mexico, Mary Frances Reza. According to Stevens-Arroyo (1998), Reza "attuned the collection to both musicality...and theological expression in the words of the hymns. The collection ranges from Puerto Rican, Cuban, and Mexican folk styles to traditional Spanish hymns to new Latino creations with elements of popular music" (p. 195). Thus the music draws on a range of Latin American origins, and expresses it in a style created by Mexicans in the United States, which is what Archbishop Levanda of Oregon had anticipated when he said (of the hymnal), "*Flor y Canto* helps bring the gifts of the past and present to us, to each other...for our common future" (Alstott 1989: p. ii).

St. Barbara's actually reflects three cultural streams: Latino culture as it exists in the U.S., particularly from Texas, the Mexican influence of recent immigrants, and the culture of the Anglo membership (which were once the majority, and still dominate in finance and council decision-making). Culturally, and particularly during the *misa en español*, the Latino influence dominates the atmosphere, ritual, and interactions. And within that Latino cultural matrix, the influence of the large number of recently arrived Mexicans is preeminent.

Music is a two-edged sword—it is one distinguishing factor between the Spanish and English masses--but also has become a way in which the two groups are brought together. Carlos, the lead singer for the Latino musicians, coordinates a bilingual mass several times a year. The mass for the Immaculate Conception was one such time. Readings and music alternated between Spanish and English. Several songs combined lyrics in both languages: *"Somos el cuerpo de Cristo,* we are the body of Christ"...Christ is revealed when we love one another..." The bilingual mass, I felt, lacked the vitality, and had only about half the number, of the average Spanish mass.

Las Mañanitas

The mariachis from Chicago had begun serenading the Virgin at 5:30 A.M. with their repertoire of religious songs. A deacon who was Potawatomi Indian performed the Native American prayer ceremony to the four winds, beginning with the east, burning a bundle of sage and stoking it with an eagle feather. The altar was surrounded by flowers and a painting of the virgin, and after mass people were going up to kneel and pray to the virgin. Some were have their photographs taken by the altar, others videotaping the entire service. The smell of food caused me to wander back into the social hall where the mariachi band started to serenade the people as they ate *menudo* (tripe soup) and eggs fried with *chorizo* (pork sausage). Many I talked with said this was the most people they had ever seen within the walls of St. Barbara's.

Las Mañanitas (literally translated "little morning") is celebrated widely in Mexico and among Catholic Latinos in the U.S. Although several Marys are the object of veneration, *La Morenita* or *Nuestra Señora de Guadalupe* is preeminent. The origins of this Mary are based on a narrative called the *Nican Mopohua*, written in *Nahuatl*, the indigenous language of the *Nahua*, one of the Aztec peoples (Goizueta 1995).[6] The narrative tells of an encounter between a poor indigenous peasant, Juan Diego, and "the Lady" of Mt. Tepeyac in the year 531, ten years after the conquistadors invaded the Aztec lands. Juan Diego was given flowers and a message for the Bishop, who dismissed Juan as an ignorant fool until the Virgin also appeared to him.

The Virgin of Guadalupe is one of the most powerful religious symbols for Mexican Catholics for a number of historical, political, and social reasons. She became one of the symbols of Mexican nationality and independence. "Were it not for Our Lady of Guadalupe, there would be no Mexican and no Mexican American people today," argues Elizondo, because it led to a revitalization of indigenous peoples who had been crushed by Spanish power (1988: 59). The Spanish and elite chose our lady of Remedies in "almost conscious opposition to the natives' and mestizos' devotion to Our Lady of Guadalupe," (Espín, in Goizueta 1995). The Guadalupe symbol is seen as belonging to the poor, as it involves the story of a poor indigenous man (whose image is reflected in her eyes). "Her olive skin tells the maestro and indigenous people of Mexico that she is one of them. In her eyes, every generation of Mexicans has seen themselves personally accepted, respected, loved and valued" (Elizondo 1988: 63).

For these reasons, "no other popular religious devotion is as closely linked to a people's self-identity, or socio-historical context, as is the Mexican devotion to our lady of Guadalupe, none other is more deeply ours" (p. 38). Guerrero asserts "that to understand the symbol of Guadalupe is to understand the essence of being Mexican" (Guerrero, in Goizueta 1995). It has continued to be evoked in this manner, as seen in César Chávez' use of the symbol during the organizing efforts on behalf of farmworkers rights in California.

What I was witnessing was evidence that here was an important symbol for the Mexican and Mexican-American parishioners of St. Barbara's, which for many years have celebrated a daybreak mass in honor of *Nuestra Senora de Guadalupe*. The previous Wednesday I had been to a bilingual mass for the *Immaculate Conception of the Virgin Mary*, but that was attended by a handful compared to *Las Mañanitas*. Extensive planning goes into this, and money is raised for many months leading up to December 12. One method was for homemade Mexican food to be sold after mass (to which I contributed frequently).

That same morning other Latino congregations were having the same celebration. In one case it has led to controversy. The multicultural congregation to the north in Lake Parish has been the scene of a yet unresolved struggle to have an image of the Virgin of Guadalupe placed in the church. The Latino members argue that she is "our virgin" and a significant part of their worship. The Anglo members resisted the use of the image inside the church, saying there is only one Virgin allowed, and have repeatedly removed the image (Jeffers 1999).

Latino Youth at St. Barbara's

It was clear to me that parents saw the Latino congregation as not merely a place where they were more familiar with the language, and where some of their traditional values were affirmed, but it was important for their children to be there as well. That was certainly articulated by Fernando. I wondered, however, "do the children placed the same degree of importance on such cultural resources as did their parents?" I would soon have a chance to find out.

Cristiana

Cristiana is medium height, black hair, and her eyes have a slightly questioning look. She speaks English with no accent. She is very polite. She was born in Texas, and her family migrates back and forth between Michigan and Texas. While in Michigan her father and mother work and live at Dresden Orchards along with her two maternal uncles, (the family described in Chapter 4.) She says one reason her family comes here year after year is the good people they work for: "Our bosses are really nice."

In Texas her dad does "odd jobs" such as video repair. Her mother works in the fields, one time I met her picking asparagus. Her sisters go to college in Texas, and come up to Michigan with the family in the summers. Cristiana plans to follow in their footsteps and attend the University of Texas, (Pan American), even though she'd like to go to

Texas A&M, but she thinks her parents would not want her to go that far. She's thinking of employment in health care, for example, in physical therapy. She says her parents strongly encouraged her to go to college: "Yeah, they told me basically we don't want you working in the fields like we are." The father, who attended community college but never obtained a degree, said jokingly that he has quite a bit of education, and so the daughters get their interest in college from him!

Cristiana has attended schools alternately between Texas and Michigan all her life. Even though she is only at Ciderville High for part of the year (from April through November) it is long enough for women's basketball season. On the team she has been playing as substitute wing, and this year (as a senior) she's a starter. Through her participation with the team she has made several Anglo friends who have been teammates since seventh grade.

I talked to her family after mass and at basketball games, and I interviewed Cristiana twice at Ciderville High. When we met for the first time at mass they were getting ready to go back to Texas in one week, but they invited me to come visit them when they return in May. During the first interview I asked her about her involvement with the church, what it meant to her:

KC: Do you go to church because it is important to you, or because it is important to your parents?
Cr: I go because my parents have always gone and I feel that I should be a part of that too. Religion is important to me. It's important to me because it's important to them.
KC: If it was an English speaking church, would you still go?

Cr: Yeah, in Texas it's like they have (different language) every other mass, one's in English and one's in Spanish. I used to go to an English mass on Saturdays with my aunts.

KC: Would you prefer one or the other?

Cr: No, I can go either way, I know what they are talking about.

KC: What about friends and relatives, do you go to meet other people?

Cr: At church? No, we just...

KC: Go for the religious part?

Cr: Yes.

On her involvement with the youth group at St. Barbara's:

KC: What kinds of things do you do there?

C: We usually discuss a topic, like we will split up into groups and they will give us something to read and we will have to discuss it. One time

they gave us something to read about friendship, a poem or something, and we had to discuss it, and get to know each other better.

When she returned with her parents in May 2000 I invited her to join a focus group of second-generation youth to discuss their involvement in the parish. Her comments during the focus group confirmed her earlier statement that language at church is not an issue for her. The issue for her is *family solidarity* ("it wouldn't make a difference as long as I come, but my parents come to this one"). Although her parents are bilingual, their language of preference is still Spanish. She goes to mass where her family goes, whether it is to English mass with aunts in Texas, or *misa en español* with her parents here. The parish her family attends in Texas, although it is conducted in English half the time, is still primarily Latino in membership (reflecting the demographics of the Rio Grande Valley.

Cristiana's indifference toward Spanish language at mass should not be carried over to her feelings about her family's ethnicity. Although she speaks English frequently at home she is not embarrassed by her parent's Mexican culture, "since its *my* culture too." When her family chooses to speak Spanish in public, she is proud of it. For someone who spends half the year in a Latino community in Texas, whose parish is primarily Latino; Cristiana does not differentiate between an "ethnic" or multicultural parish such as St. Barbara's that distinguishes itself through language, and any other parish. But for Latino youth in Michigan who are a distinct minority, *language* is linked more saliently to *ethnic* identity.

Cristiana may have a deeply personal, spiritual experience at mass, but when she speaks of her faith it is expressed in the language of family solidarity rather than in terms of personal conversion or the individual construction of self. For Cristiana, participating at St. Barbara's (or her parish in Texas) is more an expression of family solidarity than of ethnic identity. It is consistent with her high level of family loyalty that she demonstrates in other choices (for example the college she plans to attend in Texas). And while her church involvement is not intentionally out of respect for ethnic values, it nevertheless reinforces them by keeping her connected to the socializing influences of family and community.

Graciela

Fernando had told me that it was important for him that his children attend *misa en español*. I wondered if it was equally important to his daughter, Graciela. In conversations with her at their home and at church I was able to understand something about her life and what church meant to her.

Graciela is in ninth grade, short and light- skinned like her mother, and talks with a slight lisp. Her favorite subjects are English, child development, and health (because the teacher makes the material interesting). Someday she would like to be a pediatrician.

After school she typically runs errands for her parents (both work full time), helps around the house, and watches the younger brother. Having usually finished her homework at school she spends the evening watching television. Her favorite shows are *The Simpsons* and *90210*. She likes some of the music that her father likes, like Fernando Vicentes (his favorite), Selena, as well as all kinds of American pop music--Brittany Spears, rock, rap. She has a variety of friends at school, some white, some black, some Mexican.

While at her house I pointed to a family portrait and asked her about the people in the picture, and who were the most important people in her life? She said "parents and grandparents." She has little contact with her grandparents however, since they are at the *rancho* in Mexico, and she can't write well in Spanish. She speaks both Spanish and English with parents, and her Spanish is good enough that she understands what's going on at church. I asked her if when she gets older she would she take her children to St.

Barbara's. She said she would, but if she is a pediatrician she may not have much time for it.

Gracie's experience is typical of the second generation—growing up bilingual, being exposed to heavy doses of youth culture through friends, T.V., and music, and having to face the potential embarrassment of "traditional" parents. With her parents however she has been able to maintain a high level of cultural continuity. Fernando is proud that she maintains a respectful attitude toward parents and older relatives. She had spoke of an "uncle," who was really one of her father's cousins. The fact that she maintained respect by calling him "uncle" was good in Fernando's thinking, for it signifies in his mind that she embraces some important cultural values like *respeto* (respect for older family members). When her dad would come to eat lunch with her at the middle school that did not embarrass her and neither does her parents speaking Spanish in public.

Church is a place where the language and culture which she retains from her parents are reinforced, but typical of any ninth grader, she does not speak of it in that language. If she had her own children she would take them there, but admits the possibility that a career as pediatrician might prevent her regular attendance.

She sometimes attends the Spanish Friday night youth group at St. Barbara's, called *Bendita Juventud*. She says they have discussions about serious things, like recently they've been talking about abortion. Then the last Friday of the month they do something fun like having food and games. Once she told me she hadn't gone because several youth, including herself, felt like quitting because of some kids who were acting "disrespectful."

I attended one of the last Fridays of the month meetings that met in the basement of the rectory. Graciela was not there. A seminarian from Italy was conducting the meeting in Spanish, with about 20 youth and a few parents sitting in a circle. Three guys in baggy pants walked in late and sat outside the circle, speaking mostly English. The seminarian was discussing with the group the need for some kind of uniform, and they were deciding on colors for shirts with a special identifying logo. It was a lively discussion that went on for about an hour. I noticed that one of the co-leaders, a young man, seemed to dominate the discussion. A female co-leader, whom I met at the tienda just before the meeting said very little. When the meeting broke up the youth drifted over to the social hall. At the social hall a DJ and sound system were setting up for the *Baile*, which was the social activity for that evening. Later I learned that the object of Graciela's concern was the way in which the male co-leader and others tended to dominate the group.

Danny

Danny may seem to many an odd choice for including in an ethnographic study. (Talking about quiet, "ordinary" people is not considered interesting reading). But I felt that people like Danny--low profile, hardworking, dependable, responsible—do not fit the stereotype of American-raised Latino youth—and are therefore overlooked. What I discovered, however, is that Danny is typical of Latino youth in this region.

Danny was one of the first Mexican students I met at Ciderville High. He is a slim and quiet youth, handsome in a subtle, lithe way. There is something about him I liked, perhaps he reminded me of my own years in high school, shy and somewhat invisible. During our interviews he was always respectful and polite, never offering me more opinions than I asked for. I interviewed him three times at the school, and we had numerous conversations after mass. Danny drives a 1995 Chevy pickup, with a picture of the Virgin of Guadalupe on the back window (for good luck), and a figure on the front grill of a voluptuous woman. A Mexican flag hangs from the rear view mirror. During the summers he works in a packinghouse driving a forklift.

A sophomore, he's been at Ciderville schools for four and a half years. He was born in Mexico, and came to California at the age of four. Both his parents were born in small ranchos in *Guanajuato,* Mexico. Later they lived for eleven years in a small town in California's San Joaquin Valley. What brought them to Michigan were family ties and a desire to get away from bad influences in California. Dan says his mother wanted to get out of the city, and she didn't want him hanging around with "bad people":

> It was a nice town, but then there were a lot of gangs there. They built a new prison, and they started like escaping prisoners from there, it got really bad. And my uncle lived here all his life. He told us to come for a visit. So we went to Mexico [summer, 1994]and then came up here for a visit. My dad likes it here, he likes working in the fields, he doesn't like working inside a factory. Our relatives lived in Corcoran [CA], and we lived there for a half a year, then my mother liked it in Ciderville so we bought a place.

Dan's father works year-round for a fruit grower. His mother packs blueberries that end up in McDonald's

EggMcmuffins. They own a farmhouse a few miles south of Ciderville.

In early December I saw Danny at the bilingual mass for the Immaculate Conception, and he said the family would not be making the usual trip to his relatives in Guanajuato because of the possible complications of Y2K. The family maintains close ties to grandparents, brothers and sisters at the rancho in *Guanajuato*. Danny's maternal grandparents are alone at the rancho, everyone except for some on the mother's side having moved here. They call relatives in *Guanajuato* every Saturday, and every December they visit Mexico and return around New Years Eve. Last year his *abuela* (grandmother) came here. Danny recalled earlier visits to the ranchos with some sentiment:

> KC: what does it feel like to visit these places?
> D: it's fun cause you do anything you want; here you have curfews, there you get on your horse and ride around, go places...it's fun...
> KC: what about seeing people, friends and family?
> D: a lot of family comes from different places; from Mexico too...I have an aunt who lives in Choline, when we go she goes there...

Maintaining connections with grandparents is important to Danny. When I asked him who were the most important people in his life, he first mentioned parents, followed by grandparents:

> When they [parents] talk to me they tell me to do well in school so I can be someday be something in life...I want to be a mechanic, my uncle down in

Mexico has a body shop, but I don't want to do that,
I want mechanics.

He appreciates their encouraging him to follow a career
choice that he wants, and to do well at it.

Danny describes his relationship to his parents as good,
characterized by an openness to discuss what is going on in
his life: "we talk about everything; if I have problems, we
talk." I asked if he thought his parents understood how it is
to grow up in this country. He feels that they do, because
they encourage him to do what is necessary to succeed in
this society, "cause they talk to me about, you got to learn
good English to get a good job, got to get a good degree, go
to college to get a job."

Danny's friends are also important he says, but many
migrate to Texas in the winter. Fortunately one of his
closest friends does not. Isaac has been Danny's friend
since arriving in Ciderville (see Chapter 7). Unlike Danny,
Isaac's family has lived in Ciderville for several
generations working for the Dresden family.

Danny identifies himself as Mexican, although he
claims the words *Hispanic* and *Mexican* mean the same to
him. When asked if he "felt American," he said "no." He
believes he has kept a lot of the culture of his parents, for
example in his choice of music (Norteño[7]), and his use of
Spanish at home and with Mexican friends (except Isaac,
"cause he's kinda having trouble with Spanish"). He is not
embarrassed to hear his parents speak Spanish in public,
"not at all...I mean, that's the language we speak, why be
embarrassed by our language?"

I asked if he believed his "being Mexican" would be a
disadvantage to making it in this country:

KC: if you stopped acting Mexican, do you feel
you'd be successful coming up in this country?
D: no I don't think so cause I mean you need both
languages, Spanish and American, cause in every
job they tell me do you know both languages, I say
yes and they say well "you're hired", cause we need
you to inter--, to talk to other Spanish people who
can't speak English.
KC: that's been your experience when looking for a
job?
D: yeah, they ask if you know both languages, and
if yes, they give me job right there, if not...

Danny expresses no fear that being "Mexican" diminishes
his chances to succeed in this society. To the contrary, he
sees only positive implications of his "acting Mexican,"
like his bilingualism. However he interprets my question in
a linguistic way, articulating the meaning of "Mexican"
perhaps in only the sense of speaking Spanish, not in a
cultural way. Nevertheless, none of the youth had any fears
that their ethnicity would create barriers to success.

Danny's identification as Mexican, his closeness to
Mexican friends, does not mean however that he is isolated
from the wider community. He says he feels accepted by
those outside the Mexican community; he attends parties
and events among Anglos. His religious involvement is
one exception to this--he and his family attend the Spanish
mass at St. Barbara's church.

KC: Why do you go to *misa en español*?
D: I think it means something important to me.
That's the only time a lot of Hispanics get together,

do something, and then sometimes they have games, see friends.

KC: so it's important because you can get together with other people,

R: yeah other Hispanics?

KC: with other Mexican people?

R: yeah…also because my parents go, I don't like to be alone at home.

Dan's statement that *misa en español* at St. Barbara's is "the only time a lot of Hispanics get together" is somewhat inaccurate—there are weddings, Quiciñeras, dances, and Norteño bands that attract big crowds--but it is nevertheless a profound admission. The weekly gathering of a group of mostly Mexicans of this magnitude (400 – 800) people (depending on the season) seems significant to him. His perception is correct in a social sense, for where else can you find such a large and organized, regular coming together of Latinos in rural Michigan?

Almira

Almira is actively involved in the Catholic Church in Meyerton, a multi-cultural parish similar to St. Barbara's. Her father came to Meyerton from *Aguascalientes*, Mexico, via California in the 1980s, seeking a factory job. She and her younger sister came in 1990 (she was about seven years old at the time). She says she didn't want to come here: "I had my friends…at first it was strange, I couldn't talk to anyone, watch TV, or listen to the radio." Her mother worked picking apples. Other family members came up since she did--three uncles on her father's side, one on her mother's side. But most of the family still resides in *Aguascalientes*.

To complicate her difficult transition at school there was instability at home. Just after her mother had their last child the father left. The baby was four months premature, and was in the hospital a long time ("she is our little miracle"). The father was in Mexico at the time, and only came back briefly. She says it was tough, because her mother did not beg from anyone. Sometimes they had only beans and potatoes in the house. They did get some help from WIC and Medicaid.

They coped with being homesick by calling relatives in Mexico twice a week. To be with other Mexicans she went to the only Mexican church in town even though it was Pentecostal (even though her family were "strongly Catholic"). They didn't know there was an English mass at the Catholic Church. She says the church offered comfort and support. They felt welcomed at Templo Rey and got help with food and clothing. But they stopped going when people started criticizing the Catholic Church.

About six years ago they started going to St. Martins, the local Catholic parish, which had just started a Spanish mass. A deacon named Justo from Ft. Wayne came to say mass in Spanish occasionally. When he wasn't there someone translated for the priest. She feels that the situation really improved with the arrival of Deacon Manuel from Texas. Since that time her involvement in the church became extensive. She is in choir, helps with the "Good Shepherd" children's program (ages 6-9), helps teach catechism, and is one of the few youth on the church council. She has church commitments Mondays, Wednesdays, and Sundays. Her mother is proud.

She speaks of a time in her life when she became "very devout." When she was twelve she went to a spiritual retreat and was really moved by the woman speaker's message. In her spiritual life this was a defining moment: "I came to know how much God is involved with us...I was introduced to Jesus as my friend." Now she feels that something is missing if she skips mass. And it doesn't matter if mass is in English or Spanish.

I ask her about the large black cross she wears. She started wearing it after another retreat where she heard a priest from Mexico City speak about his work with youth. She had never met anyone like him; he could talk to youth in their language (even "cussed"), and then speak to older people in their language. She never had met such a "helper." The cross, she says, "is part of me."

Communities of Memory and the Second Generation

A true community is one that does not forget its past (Bellah et. al. 1996). Barbara connects its Latino parishioners to the past in several ways. Through its mariachi singers at *Las Mañanitas* it reminds people of the Mexican roots of the Latino community in Michigan. Its programs and outreach on behalf of farmworkers and students reminds the second and third generation Latinos of their farmworker roots. St. Barbara's, by its affirmation of cultural traditions important to Mexicans and Mexican Americans, acts as a cultural resource and a community of memory. Parents like Fernando recognize this and place importance on bringing the second generation into its sphere of influence—through both its events and its ethnic network.

Ainsley (1998) believes that cultural icons are important to people engaged in "cultural mourning,"-- the psycho-social process by which migrating people come to terms with the distance from family, home, and the loss familiar culture and community. Events such as *Las Mañanitas* therefore become extremely important resources that people use to move toward engagement with the new society.

People like Danny represent a new dynamic to this "mourning process," for he is like many Mexicans in the United States who are part of a *transnational* community with strong links between people in the US and Mexico. For Danny, attachments to important people and places in Mexico remains strong, and travel and communication between them is frequent. What happens during the winter months in the rancho of Danny's *abuela* is also occurring in thousands of Mexican communities. Large family reunions take place, as Danny mentioned, "people come from all over." During this time youth like Danny who are growing up in the United States become reacquainted with family and community.[8]   In a sense, people like Danny experience St. Barbara's as one of the hubs of a larger "transnational community of memory" in which cultural events are enacted in Michigan *and* Michoacan *simultaneously*. This is also very likely why *misa en español* is crowed with young single men who are not there to take communion but simply to be with "their people."

It is evident then that St. Barbara's connects Latinos to the past. But what of engagement with the present and future? Does it offer nothing for those whose destinies are yet to be realized? What does a community of memory offer to those whose concerns include making the varsity basketball team, or getting a scholarship to college, or finding a job as a mechanic? People like Federico (see Chapter 7) have recognized the need for St. Barbara's to also be a community of *engagement*. His organizing of the

Latino Advocacy Group was intended to bring students, parents, and schools together to confront issues of acculturation, discrimination, and the small number of Latinos in college. The second generation experiences this community of memory *differently* than first generation members like Fernando, who has established himself in Michigan but still retains a devotion to more traditional Mexican values. The second generation does not express the same enthusiasm for religious icons considered vital by the first generation. In a focus group with youth at St. Barbara's I discovered that they respect their parents desire to preserve certain traditions, but do not personally speak of them with the same enthusiasm.[9] Oriented as the *misa en español* and *Bendita Juventud* is toward those born in Mexico, it is not a mode of expression that youth claim as theirs.

Nevertheless, while their experience differs from the first generation, it is equally distinct from the individualist and consumerist ethos of American spirituality described by Bellah (1996). *Habits of the Heart* portrays a mode of religious involvement that finds its justification as a means of personal fulfillment, or of enhancing ones sense of well being,[10] rather than from moral imperatives. For Cristiana there remains a deep connection between religion and family. Religious involvement is experienced communally, as a natural part of family life—"it is important to me because it is important to my parents"--it is less important how it is experienced at the individual level than communally--as an expression of family solidarity. The constraints imposed by a cohesive family unit tilt her experience toward the collective-expressive mode—tempered as they are by the fact that these are

constraints *she* has chosen   ("its important to *m e*
because...").[11]

Almira demonstrates another mode of second-
generation experience. Initially her religious involvement
was a means of surviving poverty and family turmoil. As
things improve in her life, and a Mexican congregation
develops at the catholic parish, she becomes connected
there and deeply involved. Eventually she has a
"conversion" experience in which her spiritually is very
personal. Her faith becomes an integral, essential part of
her identity symbolized in the large cross she wears.
"Something is missing" if she misses mass, and "it doesn't
matter if mass is in English or Spanish." The religious
dimension, rather than the ethnic, is the more salient
articulation of her identity. This contradicts Deck's thesis
that Latino Catholics have had to turn to Protestantism to
personally appropriate their faith. Through a process of
religious education, retreats, and encounters within the
Latino congregation, Almira's Catholicism became
intensely personal, and her "testimony" is just as
evangelical as that proclaimed at any Pentecostal servicio
de oración..

The second generation youth in these Latino Catholic
congregations have charted a path that contain elements of
collective expression (festivals, language, transnational
ties) as well as personal agency (intense religious
experience, youth organizations). Their involvement in the
Latino congregation connects them not only to families and
their ethnic community here, but to many other Latinos
who are celebrating the Virgin of Guadalupe on December
12. As Ainsley suggests, communities of memory can also
be resources for engagement with the present. These
resources include affirmation of language and culture,

enactment of family solidarity, and parish organizations that address the needs of Latino youth.

Notes

[1]Percentage is from the American Religious Identification Survey (ARIS) directed by Ariela Keysar, Barry A. Kosmin, and Egon Mayer at the Graduate Center of the City University of New York in 2001.
[2]I draw on the definition used by sociologist Anthony Stevens-Arroyo (1994).
[3]The history of St. Barbara's is based on interviews with clergy (both past and present) and members.
[4]Local newspaper, 8/7/99.
[5]This is not done indiscriminately, but in accordance with what is compatible with church doctrine. Also some priests at St. Barbara's are more accepting of how traditions are practiced in Mexico than how they are conducted in the United States. For example, the more expensive and elaborate way Quinciñeras are celebrated by Mexican Americans are sometimes discouraged.
[6]My description of the narrative is taken from Goizueta who has drawn on many other primary and secondary sources of information as cited in *Caminemos Con Jesús*, pp. 37-46.
[7]"Norteño music refers to mostly rural Mexican (/American) music from northern Mexico and southern Texas most heavily practiced along a line roughly from Monterey to San Antonio. It diminishes as it extends further to the north and south, and east to the coast and west to a line between Chihuahua and Santa Fe. It is somewhat analogous to County & Western..." (Isidore Flores, personal interview).
[8]Many small villages or ranchos in Mexico are relatively vacant during most of the year because people are living in El Norte. See Suarez-Orozco, (1998) for a description of an *Oaxacan* village typical of this annual migration cycle.
[9]For example, a Mexico-born 15 year-old who had spent most of her life between Michigan and Chicago told me that her favorite religious story was that of Juan Diego, (the peasant to whom the Virgin of Guadalupe appeared). While she found comfort in the virgin as her "second mother," it was not that important to dedicate a huge festival to nuestra senora de Guadalupe. Others in the group said it was all right to have a special mass, but mariachis were unnecessary.

[10]Davidman (1991) found a similar response by Jewish women who had converted to Orthodox Judaism in that they spoke of their choice of *allowing* themselves to be *constrained* by their new religious beliefs.

[11]When other youth talked about bilingual mass, its disadvantage was that parents might not find it as attractive as *misa en español.*

Born Again in the U.S.A.

IGLESIA ADVENTISTA

One Friday night he Arturo Jr. invited me to their white, two-story house close to the church. Somewhat hesitant to disturb them, I pushed on, entered the house and found the grandmother there at the dining room table. Several small children were around. The mother was also there sitting at the table. They told me to sit down and brought me a glass of water. Arturo came in and sat down. David (a friend living with them) also came in and sat. The apartment had a small kitchen, a large central room with dining-room table, a sofa, TV, and desk with a computer. There was one bathroom and three bedrooms. Several of their friends' children were there that they were looking after. As I began to ask questions the grandmother made a few comments like, "How do we know he is not '*la migra*...he could be disguised as a church member, but a devil underneath." I told her not to worry, that I wasn't interested whether anyone is here legally or not, and that no one has to answer my questions if they don't want to. I began with questions about their history of migration and work. Arturo Sr. did most of the talking, while Arturo Jr. translated. During the conversation some noises came from outside. Arturo Jr. said it sounded like a fight; the building next door is the Red Dog Saloon. Arturo Sr. got up and locked the door.

As they narrated their story I learned that they were born in the state of *Tamaulipas*, Mexico. For about four years before coming to Michigan they began migrating between Texas and Mexico. First they lived in the Dallas area with a sister, and Arturo Sr. worked in restaurants and landscaping. They didn't seem to want to say much more about that period in their lives. Jr. added that they would spend half the year back in Mexico. The mother interjected that once the sister told them to leave ("threw them out") because they weren't contributing enough money to the household.

After that they moved to *El Valle*, (the Rio Grande Valley of south Texas). For nine months Arturo Sr. worked as a picker/cutter of cabbage (*repollo*). They heard about Michigan from an aunt and cousin, who said it was a good place to live, and they could find work. They decided to try it, and migrated to Decatur, Michigan. The first year they picked cucumbers and apples. The whole family worked in the fields. The second year Arturo worked in a packinghouse bagging apples. Then he got the job he holds presently, with a paper factory. It was the opportunity to buy a house that brought them here to Berryville. The mother added that it was God's plan, because that is how they came to the *Iglesia Adventista*. They now have lived in Berryville for two years, in Michigan a total of five years.

As I shifted to questions of a religious nature, Arturo Sr. said they attended the Catholic Church for a year. When I asked why he left he pondered the question for several moments, then asked me to repeat it. He then said there was a lot he could say. He told about going through a conversion experience, in which everything changed, things about his physical body changed. When I asked for examples he said he used to be a heavy drinker; when he was picking in the hot sun he would return each night tired and drink a liter of beer. The doctor told him his liver was so swollen it could burst. He'd be drunk three or four days out of the week. I asked his wife if it had meant anything different for her. She said that "before the family was separated, now they are together." I asked if she meant physically separated. She said yes, "They were spread out all over the place."

I first met Arturo's children--Arturo Jr. and Gabriel when I began attending Friday night "youth" meetings at the *Iglesia Adventista del Septimo Dia* (Seventh-day Adventist Church) in Berryville. I became curious about the meetings after the youth pastor explained that he often counseled kids and families who were having problems. As I began attending I noticed that these "youth" meetings also included grandparents and virtually anyone of any age who was interested.

At *Iglesia Adventista* the style of the worship service is very conservative. The hymns are in Spanish, but accompanied with only piano. Some of the hymns are translations of English songs from the standard Adventist hymnal. Their style is similar to how Anglo Adventists would have worshipped 10 or 20 years ago. Outside of language, there is no attempt to make it more compatible to Mexican tastes. But there are no complaints.

Although the style of worship is conservative, the informality of the service is intense. Children seem to float around from place to place, sometimes wandering on to the platform while the pastor preaches. The pastor asks questions to the audience during his sermon, and people answer back. People drop the formal *ustedes* form of "you" and become *hermano y hermana* (brother and sister). A family (and grammatically familiar) atmosphere prevails. After church all are invited downstairs for lunch, usually a simple but tasty meal based around beans and rice, served cafeteria style.

The level of lay participation is high. The head pastor (from Dominican Republic) also shepherds three other churches about 40 miles to the north where he lives. He therefore depends on lay members to carry out most of the responsibilities in his absence. *Campos* (farmworkers) who during the week prune trees find themselves on Saturday morning reading scripture or making announcements in front of the church; one week Arturo's brother, a factory worker with little elementary level education, preached the sermon.

Testimonios

During the Saturday morning church service ("culto de adoración") two things stand out: *testimonios* (public testimony) and children. Characteristic of many Protestant and Pentecostal sects is the time given to personal *"testimonios"* of how people have experienced God in their lives. This is a high point in the service in which a leader invites people to come to the front to speak, and young and old, all genders and classes, enthusiastically take part. Here in Berryville it is the women who are especially vocal at this point in the service. People's *testimonios* span a range of life experiences: a child asks the church to pray for her family as they leave for Texas, a grandmother gives thanks that her grandchildren were being quiet in church, a five year old boy thanks God for his brother's birthday. One Saturday Gabriel testified in front of the church, giving thanks to God about her team winning the basketball game (I noticed that her father was wearing a large button with a photo of his daughter in her basketball uniform). Some deal in the realm of the miraculous: a mother tearfully rejoices at her son's recovery from a brain tumor, or that a child with a learning disability passed a test. Some deal with human tragedy: one day I listened as Arturo's mothers testified that *Dios* had helped them during a very tough situation; a cousin in Houston had gotten put in jail, was illegal, was also in solitary confinement. Her husband and a friend had gone down to help. But this also put them in a financial bind, because Arturo Sr. had to miss work, plus the expenses of travel. Their relatives on that end said they would help cover some costs. Fortunately at this time they received their income tax return check. She gave a second testimony, asking for special prayer for a relative in Iowa/Illinois, whose tractor or truck had gone into a ditch, and the person was injured.

I learned that the *testimonios* not only inform heaven, but the entire congregation knows (if they didn't already) everybody's troubles and joys. I also noticed that testimony time held the audience's attention better than the sermon did. Some scholars of Latino religion claim that *testimonios* help to strengthen the faith of individual members (Hernandez 1999). By speaking publicly how a believer's faithfulness has been rewarded by God it encourages others to continuing believing despite difficulty or criticism.

Protestants/*Protestantes*

Berryville Iglesia Adventista mirrors a larger trend among Latino Protestants in the United States in which membership among conservative and sectarian groups has risen rapidly. *Iglesia Adventista* has only been on the scene for seven years. The church was planted by members of another larger, more affluent, multi-ethnic Latino congregation about 20 miles to the west. Some members from that original outreach effort continue to drive in and provide some of the leadership and supportive roles. Frequently there are guest preachers from the Adventist theological seminary in Berrien Springs.

The congregation draws its core members mostly from the rapidly growing community of Mexican Americans, but also has several members from Argentina and the Dominican Republic who drive in from Berrien Springs. The church has its main service (entirely in Spanish) on Saturday and holds meetings on Friday evening as well. Depending on the month there are usually between 30-50 members present on any given Sabbath. Several Mexican extended family units who live within walking distance of the church are the core members, generally helping out at all functions. There are several families who migrate to the area and attend the church during the picking season.

It is an extremely young congregation, at least half being under the age of 25. Because of this there is a "Youth Pastor" who conducts programs for children and high school age. The youth pastor will often spend some time counseling youth regarding a problem concerning school, relationships, or the legal system. Most of the high school age youth were born in Mexico, but many have spent most of their lives between Texas and Michigan. There is a large set of younger children (5 – 10 years) who are growing up entirely in Michigan, and because of their school involvement are bilingual. The older youth are mostly born in Mexico, and have spent most of their childhood there.

This congregation is new in the religious landscape of Berryville, joining a growing chorus of about a half dozen evangelical/Pentecostal or other sectarian congregations within a 20-mile radius. The Hernandez family is one of many Mexican families who have joined not only Latino Adventists but also Baptists, Jehovah's Witnesses (*Salon del Reino*), and Pentecostals.

Iglesia Adventista in Berryville is part of the worldwide Seventh-day Adventist Church (SDA), one of the fastest growing Protestant denominations or sects in the world, with a total membership of around eight million. Adventism considers itself as inheriting the biblical truths of the Protestant Reformation, but in a purer, more biblical form. Early Adventists were Millerites, a movement in the early nineteenth century that awaited the second coming of Christ in 1844. As the church evolved it maintained the belief in the immanence of Christ's return. Adventist eschatology still embodies a cosmology of the struggle between good and evil, with its final resolution being the second coming of Christ. Its belief system is essentially Protestant, with a distinctive emphasis on healthful living, the validity of certain moral codes in the Old Testament, and observing the Sabbath on Saturday.

In the "North America Division" of the SDA church (which includes Canada and the United States), membership has grown primarily from immigrants coming from the developing world (Lawson 1999). Latino membership within the SDA denomination is growing at phenomenal rates. Latino membership has grown 200 percent since 1980 (comprising 10 percent of total Adventist membership in Canada and the U.S.). At the same time the Caucasian membership is expected to become a minority by the year 2000, declining from 72 percent to 47 percent since 1980 (Lawson 1999).

Victoria

Victoria is a quiet 17-year old, with slight build, shoulder-length black hair, high cheekbones. She speaks English well. She appears quiet at first, but is confident in stating her feelings and opinions. She attends *the Berryville* During one of my visits to *Iglesia Adventista.* she was an usher. I also noticed she would never stick around after church to eat. When I interviewed her at Ciderville High her mom was in Mexico attending a funeral.

Victoria and her family are from *Nuevo Leon* state in Mexico. There were originally 11 children, but two died. Two of the children still live in Mexico, but the rest are in Michigan. The family decided to seek work in the United States when friends told them about the picking work in Michigan. When the family came nine years ago they never returned, except to visit. Once the children started school they decided to stay to let them finish. Victoria has been at Ciderville schools since the fifth grade. The father works landscaping jobs, and the mother works in a packinghouse during apple and blueberry season. Victoria helped her mom pick blueberries once and remembers how quickly she tired of it.

The most important people in Victoria's life are her family and close friends. She claims they are very close, share their feelings openly, and seek advice from one another. The family keeps in close touch with the sister and brother in Mexico, calling them weekly. Her closest friend is Cristiana (from Chapter 4), who attends the Catholic Church and migrates from Texas.

Victoria tells how she came to join *Iglesia Adventista*:

> V. Well since we were about ten or eleven, we started getting visitors from the Adventist church, and we got friends from there so we started coming... and we used to go as a family, everybody.
> K: So you had friends at the Lawrence church?
> V: Oh no, just my family friends.
> K: Family friends. Okay so some family, some of your relatives became members there before you did?
> V: Uh my cousin...and we started and then we liked it. It kind of, it doesn't, I don't, it's not like it had a lot of difference for me like being Catholic except that it's on Saturday and they don't believe in saints.

The family started attending, and at age 15 she was baptized. Eventually the parents stopped attending, but Victoria and her brother and sister kept going. Victoria says her parents are Catholic, but they don't attend church.

She doesn't see a lot of difference between *Iglesia Adventista* and the Catholic Church, outside of going to church on Saturday, not believing in saints, and using the bible more. Sermons are about the same. If she had to choose between two Adventist churches, one Spanish, the other English she would choose the Spanish one over English, even if she had friends at both. Even though she would understand it in English, she likes to hear it in

Spanish. She reads her bible, religious books, and lessons in Spanish.

When I ask her if going to church has helped her in any way she tells me it has helped her be a "better daughter," because she understand her parents better. I question her further on this point:

> KC: I've never heard that before, what do you mean?
> V: I understand how they worry about us, do certain things for our own good; now I understand why they do what they do, or like tell us not to do this or tell us not to go somewhere, because you know its not going to be good for us...why they object to some things.

Victoria doesn't see that her parents are challenged in any particular way by her growing up in Michigan:

> They are raising me the way they were raised; they are not having any trouble raising us here...they know I won't become too Americanized."

At home she speaks Spanish, and believes her parents don't worry about her forgetting it.

Eventually Victoria intends to return to Mexico and live there and go to university in Monterrey where her sister lives. She wants to go into tourism and hotel management—"I want to show everybody my country."

Although Victoria has lived all of her adolescent life in Michigan, she is overwhelmingly attached to her home in *Nuevo Leon*, and finds the city life of Monterrey much more exciting than Ciderville. She clearly, without hesitation, intends to return to Monterrey to study and eventually work in Mexico.

Like Danny, she maintains close contact with relatives in Mexico, and speaks fondly of her relationship with them:

> V: I have a grandma who says I need to learn how to cook and all that stuff.
> KC: you don't agree with her?
> V: I do agree with her. When I go to Mexico I learn how to make corn tortillas and cheese.

Like Cristiana, Victoria's relationship with her parents is very close. The place of religion in her relationship with her parents, however, is somewhat more complicated. She and her siblings attend *Iglesia Adventista* without their parents. Her parents are Catholic, but not involved in any parish. Her parents attended the church briefly, and several attempts were made to convert them to Adventism. But no longer do they darken the door of that church, or any other. Victoria, at the age of 15, made a decision to be baptized by immersion and officially join the Seventh-day Adventist church. This act of becoming a member of a different church than her parents, of differentiating herself from her family in a religious sense, sounds like a recipe for disaster. In fact these kinds of situations are favorite themes in "mission stories," where children experience a conversion, risk being persecuted and ostracized by kinfolk, but eventually, when the dust settles, win over the rest of the family. (There are many in Adventism that stridently identifies the Pope with the antichrist of the book of Revelation.) Yet when she describes her family she paints a picture of a very cohesive unit. They are very close, communicate their feelings, and give advice. There is no hint of conflict.[1]   Moreover there is cultural consonance, she speaks Spanish at home, and has not alienated her parents by being "too American."   Her close girlfriends (such as Cristiana) are Latino and Catholic.

Victoria claims that her affiliation with *Iglesia Adventista* is actually beneficial to her relationship with her parents.   Her experience there has taught her the importance of respecting the rules and desires of her parents, given her insight into why they don't permit certain activities, that it is in her best interest to respect and obey her parents.   She attributes this being "a better daughter" to her involvement with *Iglesia Adventista*, and there is no dissonance in her mind caused by attending a church different from her parents.

Victoria's case is illustrative of how the need for family solidarity outweighs denominational affiliations.   In another ethnography of Latino congregations, Sullivan (2000) observed a "pluralistic religious tolerance" among Latino families with members who had converted to Protestantism (or converted back to Catholicism), as long as these public affiliations did not erode the domestic family solidarity.   As articulated by one parishioner,

> So if they are good parents and good children to their parents, then religion is not an issue, provided, that is, that grandma can count on their help for the *posadas* [festivals]...We are Mexicans and cannot conceive of living anywhere without the support and love of a family (pp. 132-133).

As long as Protestant conversion does not interfere with Catholic spirituality that is enacted within the home, it is not seen as a threat to familial harmony.

Arturo Jr.

Eighteen-year-old Arturo Hernandez Jr. (introduced in the preceding section) has a disarming, open, and forthright manner. He's bilingual and bright, despite his tales of failure in elementary school. Arturo Jr. is typical of the youth at *Iglesia Adventista*, in that he has lived in the United States for half of his life, (and some of that moving between Texas and Mexico). He has adjusted quickly to new circumstances. Arturo is a faithful member of *Iglesia Adventista* where He regularly participates in the church service, gives testimonies, and helps with the youth. (I frequently depended on him to translate *testimonios* and parts of sermons.)

Two years ago he almost died from a brain tumor. He showed me a small photo album of pictures from the hospital, showing him swollen from the medication, losing hair, places where they put tubes, and newspaper clippings from fundraising events. I got the impression that they felt it was a miracle that he was all right now, although he has to go back periodically to be checked.

On one of my visits to Arturo's home I arrived just in time for *culto* (worship/Bible study). They were sitting around the dining table: the sister, Diego (father), David (friend/boarder). The mother joined us after I sat down. They pulled out their Bible lesson books and a stack of Bibles. (Adventists traditionally study their "lesson" during the week in preparation for "Sabbath school," analogous to Sunday school, during which they study a topic or portion of the bible; usually done before the main service.) The lesson "quarterly" (because each quarter a new booklet is issued) is given for different age groups: adults, youth and children. The quarterlies were in

Spanish, published by an Adventist office in Miami that coordinates the organization in Central America and the Caribbean. First going through the teen lesson, reading the part for Wednesday, they read a Bible verse, and filled in the answer to a study question. The younger sister was the target of the teen lesson, and the mother directed the question to her. She was not clear on the answer, but her mother and father went through the Bible verse with her several times till she agreed with them about the answer. They then went through the adult lesson in the same routine, then the children's. By this time a young boy, Mario had joined us. Arturo Sr. read the passage to him, then the Bible verse, and asked him the question, which he answered. Next was prayer. Each person prayed for something or someone. The mother asked me to pray for the *Iglesia Adventista*. They went around the circle and each person prayed in Spanish. Nearly all of this was done in Spanish. Occasionally I asked about a Spanish word and got an English translation.

During this and other conversations with Arturo Jr. I got a sense of what it meant to him to have joined *Iglesia Adventista*. He used to exchange "hard words" with his parents. "Now it is different," he says, explaining that he has a much better relationship with his mother as a result of his conversion to Adventism. High school is not the greatest joy in his life. The brain tumor set him back two grades. He complains that the bilingual tutor in the ninth grade didn't help that much, that he spoke Spanish better than she did. (When I met him once at his ESL study hall I noticed he was older than the rest of the students there.) But this year in tenth grade he's doing better. When I ask why he thinks this year is going better he says: "Because I trust in God more, he's my friend, my goodness. Today I prayed before taking the test. The students laughed at me. But I did well on the test. "

Arturo's his religious experience hints of intimacy. What he likes about the church is that his family—parents, uncle, grandmother, cousins--are here. He appreciates a small church with a family atmosphere (his cousins told me the same thing). The congregation is like a family in several ways. Strangers cannot hide in the anonymity of an impersonal crowd. Visitors are welcomed profusely and asked to introduce themselves, sometimes in the middle of the meeting. (I experienced people praying that I would return, and people testified their gratitude when I did.) The intimacy of the congregation is mirrored in the way Arturo Jr. experiences God as his "friend," rather than a stern judge or impersonal being. His religious experience actually connects him to three levels of "family"—the healed relationships with his parents, the congregational family, and the mystical sense of kinship with God. All of this combines to make it a community of healing, not in the miraculous, emotionally intense Pentecostal method, but through the communal sharing of minor and major human tragedies, and the transformation of family relationships.

Both Victoria and Arturo Jr. have been drawn to *Iglesia Adventista* through the personal ties of friends and family, and the feeling of intimacy and community of a small, tight knit congregation. This is not surprising, given the trauma of illness and the stress of migration and family instability. During the summer of 2000 Arturo Jr. and his family and uncle's family both moved to Meyerton, Indiana for better paying jobs. On Sabbaths, however, they drive two hours to return to *Berryville Iglesia Adventista*.

TEMPLO REY

*Well, my parents, they're from different parts. My
dad was born in Aguascalientes and my mom was
born in Matamoros but she lived all her life in
Arlington, Texas and my dad came up here when he
was 20 with grandma and her grandpa and, to look
for work and my mom came up to, she came up to
Fort Wayne with her dad 'cause her dad was a
minister and so they started the church in Fort
Wayne and then ..., my mom got a job in Monsanto
that was here ... and they started a church with the
Campos, with my grandpa and the Campos and
then my dad started working at Monsanto and that's
how they got hooked up. They've been here all, ever
since. That's what happened.[2]*

Two miles out of town, "just a spit" from a silo and
providentially upwind from a gentle herd of cattle, stands a
modest new white church, *Templo Rey*. Affiliated with the
Assemblies of God denomination in the U.S., which claims
a membership of about 2.3 million,[3] Templo Rey is now is
home to 300 Pentecostal believers of Mexican origin.
Although Latino Protestantism in the U.S. originally was
associated with the mainline Methodist and Presbyterian
denominations, it has recently been growing very rapidly
among Pentecostal groups.

Pentecostalism, stemming from the "Azusa Street
Revival" in 1906, is recognized as the most rapidly
growing form of Christianity in the world (Cox 1995).
Characteristic of Pentecostalism is an experience of
spiritual charisma (gifts of the Holy Spirit), in which people
have dramatic and direct encounters with divine power

(healings, liberation from "sins," speaking in "tongues"). Pentecostalism has witnessed considerable growth in traditionally Catholic Latin America, particularly in Central America and Brazil (see Stoll 1990). Its transnational networks allow missionary activity to go in both directions between Latin American countries and the United States. For example, Templo Rey was actually started by members of a church in *San Benito* Mexico, which now has branches in Washington, Minnesota, and Texas.

Although most Latinos in the United States are Catholic, Meyerton's first Latino congregation was Pentecostal. Although the Catholic parish now has a sizeable Latino attendance, Templo Rey is by far the largest and most influential in the area. (An English-speaking Assembly of God church also exists in Meyerton, which is attended by some Latinos.)

As captured in the words of a second generation member of the church at the beginning of this section, the church was started by several large Mexican-American families from Texas and Mexico who began settling here in the late 1950s through the 1970s, including a Pentecostal pastor and his children. Her grandfather, Juan Ramirez, and an uncle passed through the area while migrating to pick tomatoes. Juan was looking to settle in a town that had "more churches than bars," and he found the place he was looking for--a small Amish town about 5 miles north of Meyerton. His brother Edwin came from Texas to work for Botex Manufacturing, and later convinced a pastor in Ft. Wayne to come help start a church in Meyerton. He invited his brother who was a minister in Mexico to become the first official pastor. They first met in a house, with Sunday school classes in the garage. They raised money to purchase an old brick United Methodist church by eating together—each week a family would sell tickets and everyone would buy them, then the next week they would go to that family's house to eat tacos, tomales, and the money would go to the church fund. Then they opened the basement on Saturdays and sold Mexican food to the public. During these early years the congregation was a tight-knit, close, intimate group, being made up as it was by a small number of families and their large extended kinship networks.

As the Mexican population increased dramatically in the early 1990s, so did Templo Rey. They required a bigger church and this time the equity from the old one supplemented the taco sales. In 1995 they broke ground for the present building, and Mayor Laing was there to lift the first spadeful of dirt. Around this time Edwin left Templo was because he felt it had become too liberal in such things as the music and women's decorum. He started a new congregation in the city of Goshen.

Templo is famous for its long (but lively) services. Even the youth like Pastor Cervantes' preaching. They have a gospel band, complete with lots of brass, as well as full drum set, electric guitars and bass, PowerPoint or overheads projecting the words of contemporary worship songs words on a screen. They meet twice on Sundays, and on Thursday and Wednesday for youth meetings. Sunday nights are the well attended and members are high spiritual gear; they often have guest speakers or musicians, frequently bringing in Christian Mariachi bands like *Río Jordan*. This years' open house for high school graduates at the church social hall featured a mariachi band imported from Mexico singing both religious and secular songs.

Templo Rey is undoubtedly the most influential Latino organization in the area. Over the last decade they planned and raised money for important cultural events such as the Mexican Independence Day celebration, bringing in mariachi bands from Mexico. Mayor Laing remembers vividly that shortly after taking office in 1993 that he was invited to attend a Pentecost Sunday service at the Assembly of God church. Pastor Cervantes requested the mayor to come up for special prayer. In true Pentecostal fashion they laid hands on him and prayed fervently. Laing says he was really moved by that experience, and invited Rev. Cervantes to be on the Inter-Cultural Committee--the mayor's taskforce that tried to calm racial tensions in the town, and had a close relationship with Mayor Laing during his beleaguered tenure. During tensions between newly-arrived Mexicans and local citizens during the early 1990s the church's Reverend Cervantes was the most common spokesperson for the Latino community (see Millard and Chapa, forthcoming).

This high profile activity in the public sphere contradicts the common critique of Pentecostalism as a "mechanism for social disengagement " (Anderson, in León 1998). Anderson, a Pentecostal historian, describes Pentecostalism as a way in which protest against the social order is "transformed into religious forces that serve to perpetuate that order" (p. 164). I would argue however that what is going on at *Templo Rey* is too complex to be stretched on the procrustean bed of "domination." The reason for *Templo Rey's* preeminence among Meyerton's Latinos may be similar to that of *Alcance Victoria* (Victory Outreach), a primarily Mexican Pentecostal church in East Los Angeles. León found that there are forms of empowerment as well as domination happening simultaneously. Through personal transformation and redirecting their energies in church sanctioned directions people tap into a form of empowerment. But León adds that the daily choices available to many are often "exploitative and degrading" and years of oppression have shaped peoples ability to choose. And "if there is resistance and protest…they lie in the cultivation of ecstasy and in the critique of American society" (p. 192).

While the picture of Pentecostal mariachis may look dissonant (given the strong boundaries between secular and sacred), it may signal what León called the "locus of an evolving Chicano form" (1998). Luis León's ethnography of Pentecostal churches in East Los Angeles examined how the mysticism of Pentecostalism mixes pragmatically and arranges itself around the familiar landmarks of Mexican symbolism (found in the music and messages of mariachis), that produce a new "cultural matrix" that can "sustain what at one time would have been a cultural oxymoron: Pentecostal mariachis" (p. 174).

Second Generation Perspectives

> Mexicans are like devoted, you know what I'm saying? Like, that's the way they live.

> All my friends who are like 16 they already can go out on dates in cars. It took me three years to get to that point.

A substantial number of the Latino youth at Meyerton High attend the *Templo Rey* church. The youth leader is David, who came from Houston less than a year ago. A former "gangbanger," about a year ago he went through a conversion experience after surviving a drug overdose. Raul, the assistant youth leader is also a survivor—he almost died three years ago in a head on collision with an 18-wheeler. According to Raul, there are about 60 youth in the church, but only 20 actively involved. The youth take part in regional meetings of Latino youth from Assembly of God churches in the Midwest. Raul always manages to raise money to charter a bus to take a large group. Last year they sold 250 tamales at local factories to pay for the bus to St. Louis (this year they are selling fajitas).

On Wednesday nights the under – 19 age groups meet. Actually the first part includes parents; the music is livelier than Sundays and amped several decibels higher. After the music and announcements the youth are divided by gender into separate classes. The classes deal with more practical issues, relating to parents, dating, or focus on a biblical topic. It is conducted in Spanish, but some youth switch back and forth between English.

David

During my first visit to the weekly youth meeting I met David, and it didn't take long before he began to share how his recently took a dramatic new turn. He was born in Mexico, but spent part of his elementary years going back and forth between schools in Houston and Mexico. During this time his mom was attending an Assembly of God church. After entering a high school in Houston, he started doing drugs--first pot, then cocaine; he was in a gang. Because of his drug and gang activity he dropped out of school in his sophomore year at the age of 17. Since he had to tell his parents that he was doing something, he got a job at a factory making plastic sheets. There his supervisor was a coke dealer and they would get stoned together on the job. He and his friends engaged in minor robbery to support their drug habits, such as stealing car stereos.

One day he overdosed. He knew it was an overdose because he started shaking uncontrollably. He started thinking about his family, that he was going to die; then "God came to mind" he prayed that if he survived he would quit drugs and serves God every day. He recovered and that same day went to Mexico. He knew that if he stayed in Houston he would keep doing drugs, he needed to get away from that place.[4] In Mexico he went to church, told the pastor what had happened, people prayed with him, he cried and asked God's forgiveness. Later he came to Meyerton to live with his sister. From that point his life changed totally. Drugs do not come to his mind anymore. "I know it's because of Jesus," he says.

He sees his mission as trying to reach the young guys in the area who are getting into trouble, gangs and drugs. He plays hoop with them, witnesses to them. Once he was approached at the trailer court where he lives by some young guys who wanted to sell or buy drugs, and he took that opportunity to tell them his story; he told them "you think drugs will make you happy?" They were surprised to find out about his past. He told them "God can change your life...I've given all my life to Jesus, I was shot at but never hit." He tries to get the youth who are into trouble to come to church. They want to change but don't know how, they are addicted; some cry in front of him; he tells them the only way to change is through Jesus; he didn't want to end up like some of his friends in Houston who died. In the future he wants to reach out to troubled youth in places like Chicago.

David's story, from gangbanger to born-again missionary is a common motif of urban evangelicalism and

Pentecostalism. It is similar to that of Sonny Arguinzoni, a Puerto Rican former gang member who "got saved," kicked drugs, and eventually founded an outreach center to drug addicts in East Los Angeles (León 1998). In the 27 years since then many came into its doors like Danny, who sought liberation from drugs and gang involvement though God's help. At *Alcance* they are called the "Lazarus generation," referring to the biblical story of a man brought back to life (Leon 1998). For David, a series of life threatening events precipitated an intense conversion experience. Pentecostalism was not new to him, his mother had attended the Assembly of God churches in Houston and Mexico. David recognized that his situation was hopeless—that he could not kick drugs, and he almost died as a result. Miraculously his conversion experience helps him stop his drug use, and he claims the craving has now completely left him.

Now, far from the mean streets of Houston, he is in Meyerton. At *Templo Rey* however he finds more that an environment without the temptations of gangs and drugs. Drugs can be found in certain areas of Meyerton, and his experience has taught him how to identify dealers and customers. More importantly he has found a new purpose for his life. His life in Houston was going nowhere, a dead-end job, dropping out of high school. Now he has a mission, to reach others like himself. Personal transformations such as David's (at Alcance "the change") "enables former gang members to take control of their lives, and to imagine and live in a coherent world" (León 1998: 177). The existential postulate, or his place in the divine scheme of things has been answered—his outreach to gangbangers; Templo Rey, with its biblical moral code provide the normative guidance to keep him "clean."

Pentecostalism also provides many men a tie-in with the American dream: going into the full time ministry is respectable, and if not monetarily lucrative, commands great respect and status within the Latino community, as illustrated by the public role played by Pastor Cervantes. All this, and you don't have to be celibate either!

Estela

> Okay, I am Estela and I've lived here all my life. I have a twin sister. She's being married this summer and I have a little brother and I have a dog name Sporty and I run cross-country and track and I work as a waitress part-time.

Estela graduated from Meyerton High, the Class of 2000. She is part of the first group of children of the families that founded Templo Rey. She and others we interviewed at Meyerton High are part of the second generation of Templo Rey, that is, their parents were the first Latinos to settle in Meyerton and founded Templo Rey. I attended the open house held for her and the other graduates at Templo Rey one Saturday afternoon. A mariachi band had been flown in from Mexico, and they serenaded the guests as they looked at each graduates' exhibit. At Estela's booth there were numerous trophies from her track meets. At the regional meet this year she broke the school record for the 100 meters. Some of her close friends were there, several Anglo girls who also were on the track team. Recently a local newspaper ran a story that featured a large photograph of Estela with one of her track friends with the following caption: "...seniors Estela and Jennifer have been best friends since sixth grade. Their cultural differences have not hindered their friendship."

In her characteristically animated way she described her family history, how her father moved to the area to join his brother at one of the factories, and met his future wife at church:

> ... he went to church and that's where him and my mom met 'cuz my mom was working in the migrant fields, whatever, she worked in Washington and then these other states. Then ... she met this family...she met them somehow. So they brought her up to Indiana and she started going to church and that's how my parents met and they made me!

Cultural differences made dating and friendships more complicated. Estela remembers missing out on all those "sleepovers" with her Anglo friends:

> You know one thing that always bugged me like when my friends would be like, we're having a sleepover. Do you want to come? My mom's like, I'm like, "mom, can I go to the sleep-over" and my parents are like, "no." "Well, why not" and she's like, "cause you can't." I'm like, "we're not used to that" and I'm like, "well, why not." You know her family is going to be there. She's like, "you have your own house. You sleep in your own house!" That's one of the biggest things. I'd miss out on those sleepover. I was always mad.

One of her best friends remembers eating at Estela's house on numerous occasions, with sometimes-humorous cultural encounters: "her (Estela's) mother cooked spaghetti for us, but didn't drain it properly, it was soggy, but that's OK." Like other second generation Latinos she found herself having to reconcile expectations of Anglo friends with the more strict norms of their Mexican parents. Going out with a guy, in his car, was reprehensible to her parents:

> Okay, going on dates and the guy picking you up in his car, you do not get in the guy's car. That's just, they're like, "if you get in a guy's car, you've lost respect for yourself." That's like, you're in the guy's car and they think you're off having sex or something. I'm like, no we're not and my mom's like, well, why can't you just meet him there or if you do, they're like, take your little brother with you. I'm like, why?! [laughing]. That's the worst thing.

She remembers her mother saying frequently "but our *costumbres* (customs), don't forget our *costumbres*!."

At Templo Rey, Estela encountered an extreme moral focus that she sometimes "feels uncomfortable with." Estela's born-in-Indiana Latino friends and cousins speak of their dislike for the prohibitions against listening to popular music and going to movies:

> R: ...they think listening to nonsecular (sic) music like other religions, like other songs that's not Christian, they think...
> R: That's bad..
> R: They think it's bad. I'm like, it's not bad. It's not like, I don't think Celine Dion is going to send me to Hell or anything like that. That's just how

our church is...Like you can't, you can't listen to
secular music. You can't go to movies...girls can't
... wear pants in church.

They can't understand why their grandmothers say playing
cards is "of the devil." Their friends at the Anglo
Assembly of God church don't have the same strict rules
about music, movies, women wearing pants to church, or
playing cards. "I don't get it," they say.

But actually they do "get it." Estela and her second-
generation friends at Templo Rey consciously link the
strictness of traditional parents with Latino spirituality:

R: ... I think Mexicans perceive religion more
seriously than white people. Like for us,
supposedly it's like the way of life or it's a strict
guideline or whatever and I, when I see white
people, they're like, I don't know, they're way
different like ...Ours is like strict, you know what
I'm saying...
KC: So you think that, you feel like that's one of the
differences is you tend to take religion more
seriously?
R: Yeah...Mexicans are like devoted, you know
what I'm saying? Like they, that's the way they
live.

Estela she sees it as natural that her parent's Latin*ness*
carries over into their religious life: "The fact that it is
Mexican is not really that important, but Mexican culture
takes religion more seriously, and that is important."

Despite its strictness she describes Templo in mostly
positive terms. She likes being there, feels at home, feels

the presence of God, and likes the music and the worship service, the friendliness of the people,. She speaks highly of the pastor and his "good sermons," and says she appreciates the practical lessons, those things she has learned growing up and reminded of during church. When I asked her if she could see herself there ten years in the future, perhaps taking her own children, she say she thinks so, especially if she marries a Latino. "I would feel more comfortable that way," she says.

The youth of the *Iglesia Adventista* and *Templo Rey* come out of similar, but not identical environments. Both congregations are entirely Spanish speaking and evangelical. Both have become a religious family, a place of intimacy and community, although Iglesia Adventista is much smaller, perhaps at the stage where Templo Rey was 25 years ago. And both have parents that are concerned about the second generation, about not losing the mother tongue and respect for older values and traditions.

The youth of *Iglesia Adventista* are more strongly attached to Mexico, what some would call the 1.75 generation, having come over in the pre-teen years. *Templo Rey* on the other hand has a full-fledged second generation, Midwest-born and going through American school systems, with perhaps a visit or two with relatives in Mexico or the border areas. Most of them did not convert to Pentecostalism, but grew up "in the church." Their frustration with what they see as an unreasonably strict religion of the grandmothers is well articulated. They recognize that five minutes away there is an English speaking Assembly of God church with contemporary Christian worship and they will not be told that cards playing is "of the devil" or that dancing is a sin. Some Latino families in Meyerton have opted to attend there.

James Vieyra, who moved here from south Texas is one such person. But he did so because of a disagreement over church policy, and with much personal anguish.

The second generation at Templo finds itself constrained by both the traditions (*costumbres*) of their more traditional Mexican parents, as well as by the boundaries of a fundamentalist and Pentecostal subculture which dictate abstention from typical youth pop culture (fashions, movies, music). The potential distance between generations is extended by the conservatism of Latino Protestant churches, in that "fusing their literalistic hermeneutic with their cultural traditions" are more conservative and sectarian than their Anglo counterparts, and more focused on behavioral norms and distinctive doctrines that put them in tension with the dominant culture (see also Hernández 1995; Lawson 1998; Crane 1998; León 1998). The religious subculture of these groups acts to reinforce cultural traditions that are consistent with biblical doctrine, but will reject those cultural elements that it does not consider consistent with "God's word" such as drinking alcohol, gambling, dancing, etc.

The short-term effect has been that some denominations like Seventh-day Adventists and Assemblies of God, which had been moving toward less tension with the world, find themselves in a "sectarian drift." The second generation however is moving in a less conservative direction. Surveys of Latino Adventist youth show that they depart significantly from their first generation counterparts on a number of fronts (less is known about the actual behavior of Latino Pentecostal youth, but see León 1998; Dorsey 2000). They are less aggressive evangelistically, less strident about certain defining doctrines, more open to seeing women in the pulpit, and more likely to be engaging in such activities as dancing (still a taboo even among Anglo Adventists). In other words, the sectarian posture of immigrant Latino Adventists is not being reproduced in the second generation (Crane 1998). This could also have to do with their growing up in the church rather than being converts, and from the fact of their unprecedented upward mobility (for example Latino youth in Adventist schools are more likely to attend college than non-Adventist Latino youth [Hernandez 1995]). Although this is less true for Arturo and Victoria, qualitative research on Latino Adventist youth in other Michigan churches agrees with these conclusions, (see Crane 1997).

Meanwhile Estela and friends at Templo Rey are exasperating under the sectarian restraints of their Mexican Pentecostal elders while their Anglo Pentecostal friends imbibe the forbidden fruit of teen culture. Some youth have dropped out and resisted the pressure to return:

> ...when they're inviting me to church, like you should go to church and you should go to church. I just tell 'em like, well, if I want to go to church it's 'cause I want to go to church, not because somebody else has invited me.

Estela's cousin Sara left her uncle Edwin's church to join the Anglo Mennonite church youth group because she questioned the church's positions and wasn't given what she feels were convincing answers.

Nevertheless most have chosen to stay in the sometimes-too- strict but still culturally familiar Templo Rey. After hearing their complaints I ask them why they are still there, and they invariably answer in a similar fashion to Estela, citing the intimate atmosphere, the presence of parents and friends, the good music. Sara returned after one year with the Mennonites because they "didn't practice active spirituality" (meaning no speaking in tongues). They also claim that they will probably still be there when it comes time to raise their own children. Javier, a junior at Meyerton High, summed it up when he said "I go because I'm more comfortable with my people..." Though there is clearly an ethnic dimension to this, "my people" should be interpreted to include other[5] generational and experiential similarities—who share similar identity issues and lament about "being neither here nor there."

Notes

[1]A similar experience was recounted by a woman in Ciderville who left the Catholic parish for a Latino Pentecostal church:

> My husband is still Catholic, and we used to have arguments... Eventually we agreed not to argue about our different beliefs. He doesn't go to the Catholic Church. My brothers still go but it is easier with my family. They are not bothered by me going to the church.

[2]This and the following quotes from the youth of *Templo Rey* are from a focus group conducted by Ken Crane, assisted by Ann Millard and Isidore Flores, 5/18/00, Meyerton High School.

[3]The Assemblies of God church grew 240 percent between 1960 and 1990 (Hernandez 1999).

[4]Pentecostalism has become a familiar path out of gang life, sometimes with a tacit understanding that there will be reprisals for leaving (Vásquez 2000).

CHAPTER 7

Hot Waters in the Heartland-- Latinos and School

Teacher: Who would like to tell us what they did on the weekend?
Janey: I went to the country and saw a moo moo.
Teacher: Janey, the word is cow, not moo moo. Who else?
Bobby: We went to the city and saw a choo choo.
Teacher: You mean a train? Bobby, choo is baby talk, we use grown up language, train instead of choo choo, OK?
Teacher: Who else?
Pepito: Waving hand wildly, teacher, I have something.
Teacher: Yes Pepito?
Pepito: I read a book.
Teacher: Why Pepito, that's wonderful. What was the book called?
Pepito: Winnie the Shit.[1]

Once after mass at St. Barbara's I introduced myself to the man in a blue cowboy shirt, jeans and boots, who had been the lead guitarist. Federico would turn out to be a good friend, invaluable informant, passionate advocate for Latino concerns (see Chapter 4), and not the least important, an expert on Tejano music. We talked together many times, after mass, at fundraisers, at his house, at meetings of the *Migrant Resource Council* (which he helped found). Most of our conversations, however, took place at *Su Casa Sports Bar*.

The *Su Casa Sports Bar* is an appropriate setting to discuss one of Federico's passionate concerns—the acculturation of Latino students in the county school system. *Su Casa* is owned by a Mexican family, the clientele during the week is primarily Anglo, but on certain weekends when *Norteño* and *Tejano* bands play it morphs into a Mexican club. During our conversation rock music is blaring from the jukebox, the bar crowd is loud, and the video games occasionally emit noises. Over the din of the restaurant noise Federico told me what it was like for him growing up in Michigan schools:

> ... I started to move on, learning English and being American; but I didn't see it at that time, I didn't see it as something you had to do, it was just happening...I didn't start learning English till I was first or second grade...that's when my name was changed, my name become Freddie because Mrs. Higgins couldn't pronounce my name. And here's a non English-speaking kid wanting to learn English, so I took it. And the English word for Martínez was Martin, or Mart-*ass*, so that's how I became Freddie Martnass at school. And throughout my school years you know I still had to maintain my culture at home, my parents you know didn't know English, and again my mom and my sisters were very adamant about us speaking

Spanish so they knew what we were talking about.
And subconsciously you know I think they wanted
to, you know, keep us together as kids. Like when
we were out playing we would all be out yelling and
talking, speaking English, unless we got hit— so
they would know we were hurt! So my primary
language became less and less except for home.
And then my friends at school, you know its
circular you start doing it year after year, and
everybody starts speaking English, you get
Anglicized.

Fortunately there were some teachers interested in Federico
Martínez, one in particular encouraged him to write poetry.
Federico is very complex. He has an edge about him as he
recalls the pressures of assimilation, but he can switch
unexpectedly into a jokester. He and his band have an
endless supply of "Pepito" jokes that illustrate, with humor,
the plight of Latino students (see above).

Federico recalled memories from growing up in
Michigan:

...in '57-'58 there were like 7 families, 7 Latino
families in all of Lakeville, and now, Jeez, its like
45 percent of the population is Mexican now, or
Latino. So being few made it very easy for us to
become (Anglicized)...we still maintained our
roots, you know we dress in Stacy Adams [shoes]
and khakis,...we saw a lot of our friend who came
up from Texas and saw how they were dressed. It
think if it hadn't been for the Beatles revolution that
changed everybody's point of view about clothes

and music I would have continued to wear khakis
till now...And we still maintained that, but when
the language came we started going the other way.
And it wasn't till I was in 11the grade that I started
realizing that.

Over a bowl of what has to be the best damn *Caldo de
Pollo* (chicken soup) in the world (which just by
coincidence happens to be served at *Su Casa*) I ask
Federico for his take on what's happening with Mexican
students in the area schools:

Ken, it's like that old Stevie Wonder song, 'Just
enough for the city'. They give us just enough to
get by on. They zero in on bilingual issues, but
other needs of the population, for example, physical
or mental handicaps, are ignored. Kids are left to
themselves. They have no Latino teachers to
encourage them. The school districts want to get as
many as they can for the 4th Friday count but you
don't see the same effort being made in the spring
to recruit them when they come back. For example
in the ___ schools the bilingual kids generate
2.7million in revenue. Then they ask the
intermediate school district for the measly $49,000
in administrative funds to run the [bilingual]
program themselves. There is no regard to how this
effects the students. Latinos are not brought to the
table for planning. Decisions are made and the
plate is brought to them. When Ciderville broke off
from the ISD, local Latino leaders and 130 parents
took it to the state level at the bilingual conference

in Grand Rapids. They didn't change the decision,
but they were heard.

Clearly he feels that not all is as well as others have
suggested. Federico's story coincides with that of officials
from the Intermediate School District[2] (ISD)
bilingual/migrant education program. The director of one
such program believed that the schools that set up their own
bilingual programs have not been as successful in providing
education services to Latino youth. His program within the
ISD has over time built strong links to the Latino
community and understands the needs and culture of the
Mexican families in a way that makes them more effective.
Federico continues:

> Some Latino Ciderville graduates have done well,
> but they were not helped by the system. It didn't do
> shit for them. In Berryville you might see 4-7
> graduates per year.

Later I learned that Federico knows the personal cost of
institutional neglect. His son Mick never finished high
school. Federico feels that Mick might have finished if he
had gotten adequate attention from a speech therapist (Mick
also has Attention Deficit Disorder). Federico lays part of
the blame on the Latino community itself, which he feels
has not taken a leadership role in dealing with issues that
affect it. If it had, it could have ensured that Latino
students did better in school. I question the logic of his
opinion: "But haven't there been migrant/bilingual
programs for some time?" I ask. He says it is a
misperception that all Latinos are bilingual and migrant.
His daughter was frequently asked, "What migrant camp

are you living in?" A common perception that continues to vex many Latinos is that they are all farmworkers. Even those whose families have been out of the fields for generations are lumped together with those who swell the lines at Hardings during July and August. More needs to be done on behalf of Latino students, not just in terms of language acquisition. "Most immigrant students master English quickly, and they assimilate socially very quickly, but academically we are losing them. "

Federico, along with several professors from a nearby university, and a large number of teens, parents, and grandparents from St. Barbara's have formed an organization to look into these issues—the *Concerned Latino Parents Group*. Their project at the moment is to pair up Latino high school students with local college professors in a mentoring relationship. Focus groups of students were conducted at several churches. The research team found that many students were angry with school counselors for steering them into non-college preparatory classes. The interviews also revealed some surprises for parents—namely that many of the things facing their children had not changed since the days of their youth—language issues, communication, and discrimination. The driving force behind this initiative is that schools need to do something different for Latino kids beyond counseling and bilingual education.

Before the meeting ended Federico told the story of his decision in 12th grade to use his real name. He remembers there was something about that anglicized name never felt right, using it, he didn't really feel good about himself. When he started using his real name again, his history teacher saw it on a paper and said who is this, "Frederick"?? When he raised his hand the teacher laughed saying, "oh, its you Fred, you'll always be Fred Martinas." Federico emphasized to those youth present that people will find a way to take your dignity away—"the system will find a way to take it away, they may not even be aware of it."

HOT WATERS *AND HOOSIERS*

While sitting in on Fred Peralta's high school study hall for ESL students, I chatted with some of the Latino students about how they had come to Meyerton High. They had come to Meyerton from various places; one came from Chicago, one from Tamaulipas, one from Zacatecas, but most were from the Mexican state of *Aguascalientes*. The name *Aguascalientes* is Spanish for hot water, and the Mexican students in the ESL room jokingly nicknamed themelves "the hot waters" (the girls used the term "aguitas" or little waters). The "hot water" are part of 550 students in Meyerton's school system this year who speak Spanish as their first language, and whose families have moved to this area in the 1990s from Mexico and the border region. In 1992-93 they were only seven percent of the student population. Now one-in-five students in the school corporation is Latino of Mexican descent.

The soaring Mexican population began to be felt in the school system in the early 1990s, (at about the same time the mayor's office was noticing it). The "Minority Language Reports" began to show significant increases in students who listed Spanish as their first language. In 1992-93 Spanish-speaking students were 7.6 percent of the corporation-wide student body. Meyerton Elementary School had almost 9 percent. Two years later the proportion for the elementary school had increased to 14 percent. The middle school went from about 5 percent in 1993 to almost 16 percent three years later. From 1994-95 to 1995-1996 the Latino student population in the middle school more than doubled in number (partly due to fifth grade moving to the middle school from the elementary school in town).

The influx of Latino students has added to a school system that has been growing steadily--from 1983 to the present it has had annual increases of about 30 students. To meet this demand the corporation has plans to expand classrooms by the 2001 school year at a cost of $7-12 million. The high school principal reports that over the recent years the student increase has been about one and a half percent per year (or about nine students), with about two-thirds of that increase being from Latino students. I asked administrators whether this growth in Latino students, which must have required additional programs and staff, was perceived as a *crisis*, or just another *challenge*? The middle school principal responded that funding problems are a routine challenge in public schools. He recalled being told (by state authorities) that ESL funds were being cut while they were also getting more ESL students; "it is definitely a problem, but these kind of problems are routine." The elementary principle summed it up by saying that the word "crisis" is too strong. It is definitely a "situation of upheaval," a "unique event," but not a crisis.

The academic performance of the Latino students has caused some concern among teachers and administrators because grades and test scores lag behind those of other groups. Administrators acknowledge that tests may give an incomplete picture of how the students are doing. Students with extremely low English ability (level 1) do not even take the standardized tests; those who do take the tests encounter a cultural bias. Fred, a Bilingual Tutor and Mexican-American who grew up in Meyerton, claimed that he experienced cultural biases in the test. (How much more for Latino newcomers.) The way standardized tests are given could also be a factor: a bilingual tutor does not assist these tests, in contrast to the tests given for the regular subjects.

The school corporation (or district) has had an ESL program since the late 1980s, but the rapid increase in "language minority" students created a need to expand the program. According to the superintendent, they eventually got more substantial government funding in the mid-1990s. The West Wayne elementary, middle, and high schools have an ESL coordinator, and each school has an ESL study hall with a bilingual tutor. One responsibility of the ESL program is to test students to determine whether they should be in an English only program or not. Those who test at low proficiency levels are placed in one of four categories (one being lowest, four being the highest). Later tests determine if they are ready to "graduate" into higher levels, or out of the program altogether.

I spent several hours over a period of three weeks observing the high school study hall and talking in great depth to the ESL Coordinator, Megan, and the Bilingual Tutor, Fred. Megan is stretched to the limit, since she must rotate between all the schools. The various perspectives of students and teachers described below shed further light on how Latino students are experiencing the classrooms and social life of schools in Meyerton.

Mexican Students

When Megan comes to Fred's class at 12:30 the room is shared by students in ESL instruction and those just seeking Fred's help with their homework. Below are some observations:

> *Megan was doing the ESL instruction (levels 3 and one level 4 guy, who she was giving some extra work to). Ben didn't have any study hall students at this hour. Juan, a student a migrant family, was especially talkative. Several guys were getting ready for baseball practice (first of the season). Jose stayed for next period as well, but did some kind of learning game on the PC. They sat down to my left at the table with a guy named Padilla. I talked to Jose and a friend about their homework. Jose quickly changed the subject and asked if I knew any pretty girls in Michigan, or something like that. I said "only mi esposa."*

> *During the next hour (levels 1 and 2), a much bigger group comes in. A larger ESL class and a study hall group, all in Fred's room. This is a much rowdier group, partly because of the largeness, but they are definitely more rambunctious than earlier or later classes. Jose and another guy are walking around, and tend to speak more assertively to the teachers. Megan broke them into groups, mixing some more advanced with less advanced. Several had joined the class midyear, and were behind the rest. A young man who had not said much got up from the study hall table and sauntered to the door.*

Megan asked him for his work, he replied it was on the table and prepared to go out, she told him to give it to her. He sauntered back and handed her his work, she thumbed through it making comments. Later she told me he was almost failing. He was wearing sagging jeans, hip-hop style, head almost shaved. To my left a girl was helping Ben by taking attendance and making photocopies at the office. We chatted: she didn't need any help, I asked if she was an "aguita" [from Aguascalientes], and she and her friends just laughed. [3]

One day I am there and some of the students are taking tests. One student who is finished with his work is listening to a tape. One student who is taking a test asks him to turn it down. I walk over and ask him if I can listen. I put on the headphones and hear a Mexican rock band. I ask him the name, he says "La Tri."

Once Megan pointed out one of the students who was detained for speaking Spanish in another class. He was one of two students who were given detention slips by the teacher. She explained that under Federal Law Title VI such punishment is illegal. The superintendent is helping work it out, and at his request they have written some guidelines for teachers. Several have hinted that the language issue seems to be a sore point between a number of students and their teachers.

Megan believes that students who were good students in Mexico also good here. They tended to overcome the language barrier and catch up quickly. Fred felt that some see ESL as a crutch, they don't want to graduate out of it.

He warns them that they can't be calling him up years later for help filling out an application form.

In interviews with teachers I asked them what kind of challenge the growing Latino student population poses for them in the classroom. A counselor thought it was tough for the average teacher who doesn't want to stop the class for several students who are having difficulty with English. Teachers have had to learn how to deal with this challenge. The ESL Coordinator felt that some cope with the learning needs of these students by sending them to ESL study hall too frequently, outside of the normally scheduled ESL study hall period. She explained that when students have time in other classes to work alone on homework they often ask to go to ESL study with the actual intention of socializing with their Latino friends. The bad side of this is that ESL study hall becomes sometimes too crowded (as I witnessed), and Latino students would probably benefit more from staying in the regular classroom. She thinks teachers should check more carefully on what their ESL level is, if they are in ESL classes at all, and try to work with them in the classroom as much as possible.

Others remarked that there are some teachers that don't know how to deal with students that have any kind of learning challenge, whether it's language or special needs. This perspective views such teachers as having difficulty with any kind of special need student, including "Low English Proficient" (LEP) students. Their aversion to such students therefore should not be seen as racially motivated.

Boyd, who mostly teaches English literature and honors English, has not had large numbers of Latino students in his upper level classes. In his lower level classes he has had more, occasionally as many as 8 or 10. He said they are always courteous and respectful, although if a group of them are in class they are more vocal, less reserved, "chattering away" to their friends in Spanish. He believes that those who are lazy academically are that way because they see no use for formal education--one student had a job lined up that did not require a high school diploma.

Several teachers I spoke with felt strongly that a true bilingual education program is needed. Generally, in such a program courses are taught in two languages by a certified teacher. One elementary teacher sees students falling behind and this could be prevented by such a program. She went on to argue, from a pedagogical standpoint, the various reasons why it is needed. Students need to be firmly established in their own language to learn properly, learn the concepts in their own language and then transfer that to English. She believes it is unfortunate that many teachers and administrators use the "deficit model" of language, focusing on the lack of English skills but ignoring the "the strengths of the first language." Bilingual education acknowledges the strengths of the mother tongue, teaching students to read in their mother tongue first. It is argued that this keeps the student from falling behind in the subject matter, and better prepares the student to learn English. A high school teacher had pushed for a limited bilingual education model where one subject, such as Government, would be taught in both languages. Her idea was never adopted.

There are some tensions around students speaking Spanish in the classroom. Julio, whom I met during Megan's ESL class, had, along with a friend, been given detention slips by a teacher for speaking Spanish in class. This teacher had written down some ground rules for his class regarding foreign language usage, which stated that only English was allowed unless by special arrangement.

Megan, suspecting that this was in violation of a students' rights, intervened with the principal and was given permission by the Superintendent to research the matter further. Upon discovering that it is against federal guidelines to punish a language minority student for speaking a language other than English (when free time or time to complete homework is given), she and Fred were advised by the superintendent to draw up some guidelines to circulate to the teaching staff. A one page sheet of guidelines were circulated which dealt with translation, discipline and disrespectful behavior, and students rights of expressing themselves in any language, "as long as it is not vulgar or profane, in the cafeteria, hallways, restrooms, and during free time in class."[4]

During one of the ESL study halls I met Amalia. She is a senior at Meyerton High and headed for college with a scholarship. During fifth hour she assists the Bilingual Tutor by helping other students who are less proficient in English with their homework. She is bilingual, moving easily with both Mexican and Anglo friends. She is tall and attractive, with full, wavy hair falling below her shoulders. She is most mature-seeming for a woman her age, with a self-confidence forged through a tough past.

After her parents came to Indiana seeking work, Amalia and her younger sister came in 1990 (she was about 7 years old at the time). She says she didn't want to come here: "I had my friends...at first it was strange, I couldn't talk to anyone, watch TV, or listen to the radio." Her mother worked picking apples. Other family members came up since she did--three uncles on her father's side, one on her mother's side. But most of the family still resides in Aguascalientes. When she arrived, Amalia started in the third grade at Meyerton High:

My first day at school, I thought, was going to be the best. I was going to a new school; I was going to meet new people. I was wrong! I was scared because I was the only one that did not speak English and everyone looked at me strangely. At recess, all the girls came up to me, they circled me and talked. They wanted me to talk too, but I could not. I felt so bad that I cried. I wanted to go back to where I was from, back to my friends, back to someone I could talk to.[5]

She remembers it as a very difficult time. She cried a lot during the first whole week because she didn't know the language. Some of the kids were kind to her, some were not. There was one other Latina in her class. She would be given different assignments (coloring instead of writing). She was homesick a lot. At home she taught her younger sister the English she had learned so she would not have to go through what she did.

It took three more years before she began to feel like she had adjusted to her new environment. As she moved into high school, making friends with both Anglo and Latinos, things were better but never without problems. She sometimes found herself having to choose between loyalty to one group or the other: "It was also hard because my Mexican friends were racist, and they did not want me to talk to the 'bolillas'." I could not choose between my race and the other race because I liked them both." In high school sports she would be criticized by opposing teams for speaking Spanish to teammates. And she hasn't forgotten how someone wrote on the cafeteria table where they normally sat, "Spic go home."

To complicate her difficult transition at school there was instability at home. Just after her mother had their last child the father left. The baby was four months premature, and was in the hospital a long time ("she is our little miracle"). The father was in Mexico at the time, and only came back briefly. She says it was tough, because her mother did not beg from anyone. Sometimes they had only beans and potatoes in the house. They did get some help from WIC and Medicaid.

Her mom had a third grade education, and was willing to help Almira with her homework but really couldn't. Nevertheless she says her relationship with her mother is very good--her mother is her best friend; she gives her lots of good advice (*consejos*). She is also close to an aunt who comes from Mexico to visit them regularly.

She was never close to her father. Her dad wanted to take them back to Mexico because he felt she was becoming too Americanized. For example, he would get very upset when she could not remember certain words or translate something properly. She had no desire to return-- she had come to like it here, had lots of friends, liked their new way of life, was doing well in school, (had even grown to like school). She believes this contention over returning to Mexico was one of the reasons the family split up.

Besides church she is also involved in other volunteer activities: Charger care--community work and visiting nursing homes; PRIDE-- drug free club which helped raise $70,000 for a kidney transplant; the Soccer team; and drama--she had a part in the play "Our Town." I saw her in action when the Spanish Club performed traditional Mexican folk dances for a special *Cinco de Mayo* show in the auditorium.

"I'm Mexican-American and I'm not Mexican"

Students who had grown up in the region or were born here, whose parents had migrated here from Mexico or southern Texas, (the second generation) had a view of group relationships that differed from the views of both Anglos and newly-arrived Mexicans. Most of these second generation Latino youth, (or "old timers" as I sometimes referred to them), grew up in Meyerton with its small but strong and tight-knit Mexican community. Some grew up in nearby towns or villages as the sole Latinos of those communities. In school, many of them struggled to learn English, because they had grown up with parents who spoke no or little English. Sometimes they ended up in "readiness class" (or remedial English) because they spoke mixed English mixed with Spanish. Sometimes they were given assignments separately from the rest of the class and below grade level, such as coloring books. Sometimes they were told to wait for the teacher to explain the subject after class.

As they grew up they encountered discrimination. "This is a white man's sport," a Latino student was told who managed to make the basketball team. A Latina spoke in a focus group of the lunch table where she and some other Mexican students sat. One day when they arrived, they found written there, "go back to Mexico." Nevertheless they managed to find acceptance with some of the white students, and many counted one or a few white students among their close friends.

Their concern, however, was not only how they were perceived by *Anglos*. Their narratives revealed their frustration with being looked down upon by the more recently arrived Mexicans. An example of this is Rosa, who was born in Texas and grew up in the only Latino family in an Amish town 10 miles from Meyerton. She feels the newer Mexicans see her as "just a white girl."

> ...I'm just a white girl, you know... I'm not with Mexicanos, I'm just a white girl and that's still hard right now. Right now it's just like oh, well, Mexicanos, they don't treat me as a Mexican because I'm not Mexican but then white people are like, well, I'm not a white, you know. I'm not American. So I'm right in the middle. So I'm not there and I'm not here, you know, so it's very hard for me...You know, you don't speak any Spanish so you're white. You're an Americana and that's what they call me, like Gringa or that kind of stuff. Oh, that gets me so mad... I'm Mexican-American and I'm not Mexican and I'm not American. I just, right there in the middle, you know, and it gets me so mad because like they're, they think that I'm white and I'm not and they think I'm Mexican and I'm not and, oh, that gets me mad. That gets me really, really, really mad...

They believe Mexicans see them as no longer truly Mexican, but Americanized ("gringa, "white boy," "wannabe," "bolillo(a)" or "preprancholo"—a combination of "prep," "ranchero," and "cholo"). Having Anglo friends makes them suspect in the eyes of the Mexican students. They find this experience of rejection by those of their same ethnicity troubling. "You're like racist against your own race...if we're all Mexicans, how can we be racist against Mexicans?"

Conversely, their judgment of the recently arrived is not complimentary either. They joke about the yokels from the *ranchos* in their boots and jeans, women in shorts and high heels, and trucks with names on the back window, lots of fuzzy ornaments inside, 20 antennas, and "guys wearing too many gold chains and not enough deodorant." They are not *bien educados* (polite). The women complain of the stares and comments made by the men. "You can't wear a skirt because all the guys will be there staring at you." They speak of being embarrassed by them, and that it perpetuates a stereotype that all Latinos are like that.

On the other hand, they also have empathy as they watch the newcomers go through experiences similar to theirs in the classroom. They notice when teachers send the Mexican students unnecessarily to ESL study hall. They watch painfully as their Anglo friends make disparaging comments, as discussed by one Latino student.

V: Antonio came in and they're like saying, "Oh great, another one that doesn't speak English." Then he's like, "I speak English," and they're like, "Oh, oh, you do." And it's like, I don't know, I feel like, I feel bad inside, you know, but it's like I want to say something but at the time I'm like, "No, I can't say nothing 'cause then they'll talk about me." ...I usually end up saying what I feel, but I get in trouble...

E: ...Or sometimes, the teachers say something that like, gets to you. They're like, "Other Mexicans are like..." And it's like, "No, I'll just keep it to myself," you know.

K: When you say it gets to you, is it...

E: It makes you feel bad...

> K: Is it said towards you as a, as a person, as a Mexican...?
>
> E:...'they're not racist towards me 'cause I mean, 'cause they already think I'm white, you know, but like sometimes I'm just like, I feel bad 'cause I mean, they're like, they're still my people, you know, and I feel bad 'cause my, all my, my parents are from Mexico and everything and I'm just like, I'm like, you know what, just put yourself in, I always just tell people to put themselves in their shoes and just, how would they like to be, if they were treated that way, people wouldn't appreciate it so, I don't know.

They also resent the way they were treated as de facto teacher's aids for newcomers.

> Also, in sixth grade, I guess some teachers aren't patient enough 'cause in sixth grade, they, two new Mexicans came in and they give 'em to me right away, tell 'em to sit by me and I would translate for 'em because they just didn't want to bother with that and it was my job to teach 'em actually and I guess some teachers aren't patient enough. The teachers thanked me and all but I kind of was thinking like, I wish we could work individually and we could get a little bit slower with them but still, you know, she teach them, instead of she making me teach them.

The arrival in the mid-1990s of large numbers of new Mexican students from Mexico and the border states has created a paradoxical situation for the second generation.

Being bilingual and having white friends they are considered the "cool Mexicans" by Anglo students. Showing solidarity with the newcomers makes them targets of the same "spic go home" remarks that characterized the backlash from some Anglos to the growing Latino student body. During the racially charged middle school years they found themselves in a difficult position:

> Yeah, the guys were gonna fight the Mexicans 'cause something had happened and then the white people were gonna fight the Mexicans and even their girlfriends were gonna fight the other guys' girlfriends and I remember 'cause like my friends were like Americans, you know, and I'm just like, oh my, and it made me sad 'cause like I feel like I have to choose between people and I hate that. I'm like, it just makes me sad.

On the other hand, having white friends makes them suspect in the eyes of newcomer Mexicanos who have initially kept to themselves.

By the late 1990s they found themselves part of a large minority of Latino students. Both the well-established and newcomers alike began to see themselves part of a larger Latino presence. As ethnic solidarity began to override mutual in-group suspicions the second generation experienced a sense of group power: "It's better now; they [Anglos] always talked against us, but now there are more of us and they're afraid." Along with power came a heightened sense of ethnic identity and pride, articulated when Latinos competed at sporting or academic events.

Once I went to a track meet... When a Mexican
wins first place and stuff, I don't know why, I'm not
even winning it, but when I see a Mexican getting
the first honors, second honors, beating all these
people, I guess I feel proud.

The net result of this greater sense of power and pride
meant that social success was less dependant on
assimilation into Anglo student culture. Latino students
could now impose their own boundaries, "We don't let
them [Anglos] in ...you talk to Hispanics because you talk
about more of the same stuff."

Schools and Segmented Assimilation

A large portion of this study was conducted in school
settings because of the important role they play as agents
of acculturation for children of immigrants. "It is in school
settings that immigrant youths come most directly in
contact with native peers – whether as role models or close
friends, as socially distant members of exclusionary
cliques, as sources of derogation and discrimination, or of
peer acceptance" (Portes and Rumbaut, forthcoming).

The experiences of Latino students at Meyerton High
demonstrates the eroding effect that high school can have
on retaining the mother tongue. In their early years they
were given numerous disincentives to maintaining their
fluency in Spanish. The consequences of this reality is
captured in recent analysis of ethnographic work on
immigrant children in school:

...children are caught in a fog where confusion
about self-identity and disorientation in school

couple with a growing stigma about speaking a foreign language. The result is limited bilingualism, at least in the short run, as imperfect English acquisition accompanies the rapid loss of the language brought from home. Some actually remain in this situation, which for children represent a telling indictor of dissonant acculturation – increasingly unable and unwilling to communicate with parents in their native language, while still lacking full English fluency (Portes and Rumbaut 2001: 130).

The experience of the Meyerton High's second-generation Latino students is common among non-white second-generation youth who eventually encounter a racialized society in which they experience pressure from both co-ethnics and peers outside their group. Meyerton's "old timers" found themselves in the "fog" of confusion about their bicultural identities as second generation Latinos in an increasingly polarized community. Federico describes their dilemma as the "abobe-brick syndrome"--the second generation is caught between the Mexican (abobe) and the Anglo (brick) side. He believes that it is at this point that "we are losing them," -- families are experience division as youth tend to resolve the tension of being in the middle by going to over to one or the other, usually opting for Anglicization. "Youth need to know that they can be both Mexican and American, but there is nobody to tell them that it's OK to be both."

These "identity juggling acts" are echoed from other U.S.-born, Spanish-speaking youth throughout the country, such as 17-year-old José Mendoza, "a Dominican who is not black enough for many African Americans, not light enough for most Hispanics, and is advised by his parents to "marry light" (Portes and Rumbaut 2001).

As Federico suggested, one common response is trying to downplay the differences they perceive themselves as having to reduce conflict through assimilation. However student reactions to Proposition 187 in California point to the possibility that perceived affronts to ones ethnic group may heighten ethnic solidarity and self-consciousness (Portes and Rumbaut 2001).

Another negative aspect of assimilative pressure in schools is faced by families who settle in socio-economically marginal communities. Becoming "American" in this context does not necessarily lead upward into the middle class, but downward into the urban underclass. Adaptation (and survival) in this context means adopting the leveled aspirations of neighboring minority youth with their corresponding "adversarial stance" toward dominant "white" society (Portes and Zhou 1993).

The classic study by Matute-Bianchi (1986), is frequently used to illustrate this pattern. In her study of Mexican and Japanese students in California she observed many U.S. born high school students adopting a *cholo* identity, which disparaged attempts at academic success and postured itself in opposition to the school establishment. This is argued to be an adaptive strategy to protect self-worth, since taking the accepted route of education as the ticket to the American dream is seen as hopeless, and would only lead to failure and humiliation. Other studies of Mexican-American youth have identified higher levels of preoccupation with failure and bleaker outlooks toward the future among the U.S. born (Suárez-Orozco and Suárez-Orozco 1995).

In light of the fact that psycho-social adaptation of immigrant children is complicated by the vast and subtle complexities of what it means to be an American, it is truly remarkable what Meyerton's second generation Latinos have accomplished. First they were able to avoid the plight of "limited bilingualism"[6] as most were fluent in English as retained the ability to at least verbally communicate in Spanish with parents and grandparents. Secondly they are aware of their unique, albeit perplexing situation of being part of both Mexican and Anglo worlds, but they have chosen not to resolve these tensions by lessening their differences with Anglos, despite a backlash among some Anglos to the growing Mexican population. Nor have they embraced the icons of popular youth culture to the extent that it has marginalized those values that parents reverence, including language. Last, they were also able to avoid the path of dissonant acculturation that rapid Americanization can bring about (Portes and Rumbaut 2001; see also Waters 1996). None of those interviewed believe that there are any serious barriers related to their race, language or ethnicity-- to achieving the American dream. While not all see themselves as college-bound they value education and view the future with much optimism.

It should also be pointed out that Meyerton is not Brooklyn, San Diego, or Miami--cities where most of the second-generation research is being conducted. A Midwestern, semi-rural community with a robust economy, its high school is not beset by the violence, drug abuse, and decaying infrastructure that are daily realities for many urban high schools. Many parents I spoke with came to this community to find better educational opportunities for their children (as well as to take advantage of jobs and reasonable housing). What both youth and parents discovered was that along with their positive qualities, these schools had their own set of challenges for Latinos associated with language, assimilative pressure, and racial hostility.

Notes

[1]As told during an interview with Guillermo Martinez.
[2]The ISD provides teachers to county schools for special programs, such as Migrant Education.
[3]Field notes, 2/28/00, 5/24/00.
[4]Staff Newsletter #5, March 17, 2000.
[5]Amalia H____, "What it's like to fit into two cultures," local newspaper, 5/4/00.
[6]Limited bilinugualism is a condition of limited proficiency in *both* the mother tongue *and* English (Portes and Rumbaut 2001).

CHAPTER 8

Intersections of Faith, Family, and Ethnicity

While the individual experiences of these youth are worth examining in their own right, I believe that their experiences are key in understanding how the ethnic church shapes their life trajectory--their sense of identity and self-esteem, relationships with parents, and success and failure at school and work.

Latino youth are a large and fast growing group, and it is important to understand how religion can help them negotiate the difficult transition to successful adulthood and meaningful participation in society. The tough environments and choices facing Latino youth--drugs, ultimate values, confusion about the future, moral values, educational advancement, presents one of the greatest challenges to their religious communities:

> Survival among Latinos requires this young generation to confront issues of language maintenance, bilingual and multicultural education, and an end to welfare dependency... they will not only affect social change, but also alter much of U.S. Catholicism in the process (Stevens-Arroyo 1998: 121).

What Stevens-Arroyo says about Catholic youth applies equally to Protestants. One of the most critical tasks facing

Latino churches is how to enrich and strengthen the lives of second-generation youth.

SELECTIVE ACCULTURATION AND THE ETHNIC CHURCH

> *...but you have to wear dresses. If we wear pants it's like, 'oh my gosh'. And they always talk about us ...they can mind their own business.*[1]

Despite the many continuities with their immigrant parents, the second generation still experiences these religious communities in their own unique way. It is not surprising then that they should not fully connect with a religious community that in some ways is more oriented toward the immigrant generation than to their concerns. They typically find less significance in the cultural icons that are vital to parents, or seek different modes of expressing their significance. For example, the girl whose favorite story is the Virgin of Guadalupe also says that a special mass for her is *unnecessary*. The Pentecostal youth whose parents discouraged secular music played in Christian Tejano bands with names like *Los Elegidos* (*The Chosen*, from a verse in the New Testament).

These differences are to be expected, since their lifeworlds and experiences of growing up in the Midwest are different from their parents; parents may teach them to appreciate the older *corridos (ballads),* but they grow up grooving to the sounds of hip hop and rock. Growing up bilingual they move in a wider social universe, have Anglo and African-American friends, eat at Wendys, run in track meets with Anglos, and are avid consumers of the pop youth culture of America (both Jay-Z and Ricky Martin).

Given these realities, is there any evidence in the lives of these youth that Latino congregations can facilitate successful transitions into adulthood without "dissonant acculturation" and its attendant loss of social control and rift between parents and children? If so, by what mechanisms is this being accomplished?

While they take a more liberal view American culture than their parents, these youth could still be considered quite conservative. They may scoff at the prohibitions against movies, dancing, short skirts, and secular music, but they take seriously the church's stand on premarital sex, drugs, alcohol, and smoking. Whether they like to admit it or not their involvement in the ethnic church mitigates certain risk behaviors common among their non-churched peers. Sara, for example, reflects on her time at church as a way she was "sheltered" from "worldly" influences. Even though she did go through a short wild stage, she believes her church involvement prevented her from really living a "crazy" life. What follows below is an analysis of the mechanisms involved in how Latino churches facilitate a path of selective acculturation.

Support for bilingualism

One key to achieving selective acculturation is through maintaining fluency in the parent's language, since "fluent bilingualism makes possible better inter-generational communication because children can talk to their parents *regardless* of the latter's English ability" (Rumbaut and Portes 2001: 134). The CILS study also found that it was more bilingual Latin American second-generation youth who had the most cohesive families as well as the lowest levels of parent-child conflict.

The parents in these churches felt it was important to be vigilant about speaking Spanish at home in order to preserve relationships, not only between parent-child, but with grandparents and Spanish speaking relatives here and abroad. The youth in the preceding narratives, despite intense pressure at school to acculturate rapidly, most survived their school experiences with the mother-tongue more or less intact. Although they have varying proficiencies in Spanish, most of them speak it well enough to maintain close ties with parents. Some of them specifically pointed to their church involvement as strengthening their bilingualism, since they were "forced" to read their Bibles in Spanish. Admittedly, if a person is not fluent in Spanish, or Spanish is discouraged at home, going to church is not going to make her bilingual. For the youth in this study however, religious involvement appears to have been a *key institutional support* for the maintenance of language.

Even in rural areas, church is not the only place where Spanish is spoken and read. In Meyerton, for example, Spanish is spoken by a growing immigrant population for whom Spanish is their first language, and who meet in shops and parks. They are also served by media such as Spanish newspapers and radio stations originating from cities in the Midwest, as well as cable television from Chicago and Miami. (When Arturo's mother finishes studying her bible in Spanish, she relaxes on the couch and watches soap operas on *Telemundo*). Latino parents, even in rural areas, have the advantage over groups such as the Vietnamese because greater support for Spanish usage outside the home.

The second generation of Latino congregations may be unique among ethnic groups in that they have a strong sense of ethnic pride and place a high degree of value on their mother tongue. The CILS study found that most Latin groups had lower proportions of youths who reported being embarrassed by their parents (Portes and Rumbaut 2001). In Ebaugh and Chafetz's (2000) study of immigrant religions in Houston, it was the Latino youth (including second generation) who stood out as striving to maintain the language. A similar phenomenon was observed at St. Barbara's, where language assumed salience as a symbol of Latino solidarity that bridged intra-group differences (social class, generation, national-origin). Latinos that attended the English mass were often criticized by their peers for doing so, and Latino youth would speak English around other Latinos, but switch to Spanish as Anglo kids entered the room.

Inter-generational Relationships

The negative effects of assimilation, despite its assumed benefits under the old logic, come from the breakdown in inter-generational relationships. The role that the ethnic church played in preventing this kind of dissonance is worth looking into. All of the youth of this study speak of strong relationships with parents, whom they can openly talk with about their lives even in cases where they have different religious affiliations. They are not embarrassed by their parents, although some considered certain restrictions as "old fashioned" (for example dating or sleepovers with friends). Given the importance that Latinos place on familial relationships, it is no surprise that Latino religious identity is also cast in terms of *familia*. When asked "What is Hispanic about your congregation" people will say "we are *familia*." (Armendaríz 1999: 242). Latino congregations are like extended families, with open displays of warmth and affection, with people referring to each other as *hermano* (brother) and *hermana* (sister). Latino congregations are therefore places where the *cultural* notions of family are enacted and celebrated.

For the teenager whose favorite religious story is about Juan Diego and the Virgin of Guadalupe, the ethnic congregation is a place where she can celebrate her love for the Virgin alongside her parents. Thus the church (to the extent that youth also find meaning in its symbols) fosters cultural continuity between generations.

Latino congregations, especially smaller ones, often consist of groups of extended families. Almost all the parents of these youth got introduced at church. Thus kinship groups were incubated here, ("that's where they met and then they made me") and clusters of families formed around these congregations. Church was a place where large extended families could regularly reunite.

The common thread that weaves these eight Protestant and Catholic youth together is the way in which their respective religious experiences have implications for important family relationships. For Victoria (who converted to Protestantism), her faith community reinforced respect for the role and difficulty of parenting (even though her parents remained Catholic). For Cristiana her religious involvement was implicitly a way to enact family solidarity. For Arturo his religious experience meant healing the relationship with his mother, mirrored in the intimacy he felt in the church family (we are all *hermanas y hermanos*). For Danny it was a transnational bridge to his family in *Guanajuato*.

Ethnic Solidarity and Spatial Considerations

...its not because I'm racist that I go to Templo, its just that I'm more comfortable with my people[2]

In reviewing the experiences of other immigrant groups we see that settlement outside of communities of high co-ethnic concentration decreases the possibility of involvement in ethnic institutions. Rapid "straight-line" assimilation is more prevalent where families are not integrated into strong ethic communities. In the case of Indian groups who were geographically dispersed in suburbia it was through religious institutions that they resisted acculturation. Likewise for Latinos in these more rural, geographically dispersed communities, religious congregations are one of the key places of face-to-face interaction, and it is not unusual for families to drive for over an hour to attend St. Barbara's. Churches like St. Barbara's and Templo Rey are the largest regular, public meetings for Latinos in the region. This should not be underestimated, remembering that for Vietnamese youth it was social interaction and networking rather than language instruction that facilitated their integration into the ethnic community (Bankston and Zhou 1996). Likewise the Latino church, especially where it provides the primary social space for ethnic groups, is one of the most important mechanisms for integration into an ethnic community.

While religious institutions also offer practical assistance in social mobility they have emerged primarily as a means for a Latino minority to celebrate their religion in a culturally familiar fashion. Latino churches are often quite diverse in terms of race and national origin. At least one of the congregations of this study included people of

Germanic ancestry from South America and people of African descent from the Dominican Republic, as well as its core membership of Mexican origin. Elsewhere I have witnessed congregations in which in the course of one hour there were people leading out who were from Peru, Puerto Rico, Dominican Republic, Honduras, and Mexico, who were of European, Mestizo, and African ancestry. Congregations of primarily Mexican members are often diverse along regional lines (see Sullivan 2000). Such congregations are able to forge a common cultural identity based on the language and similar values about family relationships, respect, and hospitality.

The statement by the youth about being more comfortable with "his people" strongly suggests that it is a sense of ethnic solidarity, based on the shared experiences, common culture and language, and feelings of *familia*, which draws Latinos into religious congregations. For Latino youth in small Midwestern towns, who are part of a spatially dispersed minority, a community of memory affirms the peoples' beliefs and traditions. It is a place for the second generation to enact the Latino side of his/her identity. You will recall that Cristiana is comfortable attending an English mass when she is living in her primarily Latino community in south Texas. In parts of rural Michigan and Indiana, however, it is through ethnic churches that one can find the comfort and affirmation of "my people."

Mechanisms of Ethnic Socialization

Is there any evidence in the preceding chapters of this work that they can facilitate successful transitions into adulthood without "dissonant acculturation" and its attendant loss of social control and rift between parents and children? If so, by what mechanisms is this being accomplished?

There is strong evidence therefore that these youth are on a path of selective acculturation, indicated by their bilingualism, their regard for parents, and their appreciation (at times reluctant) of the cultural values important to parents. I believe there is evidence that involvement in Latino religious institutions has fostered this outcome. The primary mechanisms for this appear to be the ethnic network effect and extended family structure of Latino congregations (See Figure 1).

Latino religious institutions are a fundamental way in which a geographically dispersed community comes together on a regular basis, and that in the process of enacting religious meaning it also carves out public space for its language and tradition. They are a further support to the maintenance of language, and a place where cultural values are communally celebrated. Young Latinos interact with one another and with extended family.

The process of ethnic socialization, however, is *tied inextricably* to *familia*. Ethnic socialization was effective *when the congregation itself was an extention of the family*. It is through the matrix of family that these youth experienced their religious socialization, which explains *why* the language of family dominated their narratives. The church was an effective ethnic socializer to the extent that it could support strong influences that were already at work in these families. In turn it re-enforced family solidarity and respect for parental guidance. Latino religious institutions, therefore, were effective in shaping the lives of youth because they functioned as supporters and extensions of the family--the primary "crucible" of ethnic socialization (see Rumbaut 1994).

Notes

[1]Focus group of second generation youth of Templo Rey.
[2]Javier Gomez, on whether he preferred a Latino Pentecostal congregation to an Anglo congregation (interview 6/28/00).

Figure 1: Mechanisms of Ethnic Socialization

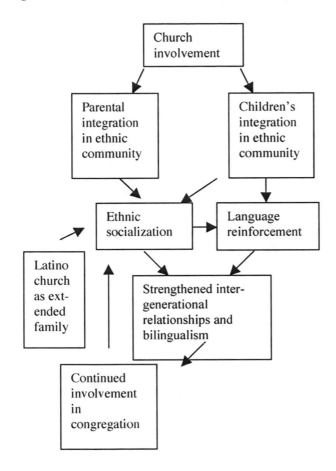

CHAPTER 9

Conclusion

Scholarship is in the process of conceptualizing new models of acculturation and ethnic identity for immigrant children. We have only begun to scratch the surface, however, as it concerns the role of religious institutions. I have endeavored here, metaphorically speaking, to *scratch further*.

The preceding ethnographic narratives and analysis are an attempt to understand the experiences of Latino youth in three different religious congregations. In this chapter I will sketch out a picture of the second-generation that reflects the experiences of youth in these Latino congregations as contained in their narratives about family, school, and religious experience. Secondly I will summarize and emphasize the conclusions drawn from this study.

An Emerging Profile of Latino Youth

All of these youth in this study are of Mexican origin,[1] some have parents who were born in the borderlands, while other youth migrated in their elementary school years. Some represent the more recent migration of Mexicans to the Midwest. Some of the Latino religious activists represent an American Latino community that has existed in the Midwest for three generations. As such they bring a diversity of histories, indicative of the plurality of Latins in this country. They have the common feature of all being involved in varying capacities with a religious congregation that is Latino, primarily Mexican.

The second-generation youth of these congregations are children of working class and working poor parents. Many of these parents were at one time farm laborers, and some have moved into better paying manufacturing or processing employment. They have chosen to settle in rural areas of Michigan and Indiana, away from urban problems, where job opportunities and educational opportunities are considered better than in California, Chicago, Texas, or Mexico. The schools their children attend, while of fairly high quality, rarely affirm the language and culture of Latinos, and linguistic acculturation is rapid. The parents have consciously acted to mitigate the influences that erode mother tongue and tradition by encouraging appreciation for culture and language in the home. Another support to their efforts involves the regular gatherings of Latinos in religious communities of memory. Parent's hope to that youth will be brought into regular contact with others of similar ethnic origins, and guided by the familiar markers of collective expression.

Why they stay--it's all about family

Like their parents, the youth also experienced their religious action as a form of ethnic integration and solidarity, as a way of being with "my people." Unlike their parents, however, it was a place where they could express both ethnic and American identities, (for "my people" includes other bicultural second generation youth), and where they were creating modes of expression growing out of their American experience.

Involvement in these congregations did not inoculate the youth to the inevitable risks of growing up American. Linguistic acculturation has been rapid, and many have Anglo friends from their sport and club involvements. The attitudes and choices of the second generation reflect a higher degree of individualism. Certainly their experience growing up in the United States has shaped their worldview and is reflected in more individual-centered views. This resulted in differences and disagreements between youth and parents, youth and clergy, and between newly arrived and old timers. Some have been bold enough to challenge parents and religious leaders about practices and beliefs.

While some would argue that in general the second generation has found the ethnic church to be too stifling and strict, and has no intention of staying very long, I would suggest a different scenario. Certainly many have left despite their parents' edicts and desires. But a significant number have chosen to stay in the ethnic church for multiple reasons--out of a strong sense of ethnic pride, a desire to be with "their people," family cohesion, and because they experience the congregation as a kind of extended family. Aside from the spiritual experience (which for some was intense), the greatest overall salience that the churches had for youth was that they were extensions of *familia*. These families were able to stay strong despite their generational differences, that is, they were not torn apart differences in worldview and language ability. This makes inter-generational involvement in ethnic institutions a *natural consequence* of family cohesion.

Congregations and Family Support

As such the congregations were able to aid in the process of
ethnic socialization already being carried out by families.
These families were effective agents of ethnic socialization
because they had high levels of cohesion and low levels of
inter-generational conflict (the two are negatively
correlated), both highly correlated with *selective
acculturation*. The congregations and families were in a
mutually supporting relationship. Both family and church
contributed to high levels of bilingualism, associated with
lower levels of inter-generational conflict. Family
solidarity and respect for parents made it more likely that
youth participated with parents in churches. In turn, the
networking effects and teachings further supported the
ethnic socialization process, affirming the importance of
family and parental roles. Latino religious institutions,
therefore, were effective in shaping the lives of youth
*because they functioned both as supporters and extensions
of the family.* Nevertheless, as Portes and Rumbaut
observe, "it is not acculturation per se but the *form* that it
takes that leads to different degrees of estrangement
between immigrants and their children" (2001: 193). The
family-congregation nexus combined to shape a more
selective *form* of acculturation that maintained a high-level
of family cohesion and linguistic-cultural continuity.

Latino Youth—The Exception

The youth did not see their involvement in an ethnic
church, immersed in its language and surrounded by
immigrants, as an impediment to making it in America.
None of them anticipate any problem with achieving the
American dream because they are Mexican and Spanish

speaking. To the contrary, they see competitive advantages to being bilingual. The recent RENIR project in Houston reveals that despite strategies of reproducing ethnicity and language many ethnic congregations are generally not successful in retaining a substantial and bilingual second generation. Most of the Asian congregations have a sparse and more conflicted second generation with respect to language, with higher levels of embarrassment about parents culture and lower levels of bilingualism. Thus "Hindu youth are conspicuous by their absence from temple" for without a knowledge of the language they cannot meaningfully participate (Ebaugh and Chafetz 2000: 427). The study mentions Korean youth, fluent in the language, denying to Anglo friends they have any knowledge of it. Even English language events targeting the second generation are poorly attended. Often spatially dispersed, these youth do not have the same matrix of supports that maintain bilingualism among Latino youth.

Most recent ethnographic studies identify Latino youth as the notable exception to this pattern. Many Latino congregations have a substantial second generation with high levels of bilingualism. The Latino youth in these studies presents a profile consistent with that of the CILS study where Latino youth were found to be least embarrassed by their parents' ethnicity and more likely to be bilingual than other nationalities (Portes and Rumbaut 2001). Here we see a remarkable consistency between this study, which looks at the religious side of the Latino second generation, and large-scale studies such as CILS. In both there are similar patterns of success in maintenance of language and bicultural identity.

A Place at the "Multicultural Table"?

The positive relationship between religious involvement and selective acculturation of Latino youth congregations confirms Warner's view that religion has increased the diversity of our society rather than facilitated "incorporation" of immigrants into the mainstream of some kind of homogenous denomination. In the current national climate in which ethnic identity is valued it is understandable to see religion as a means for the second generation to assert its ethnic identity, or in the words of Kurien to "take their place at the multicultural table." Naturally this may be truer in Los Angeles and Houston than in Ciderville and Meyerton. What of communities where "no multicultural table" exists?[2]   In the small rural schools and communities where these youth live and move the local mantra has always been "they need to learn English," and "they need to adapt to *our ways*." Local fears of Mexicans "not integrating" into "our way of doing things" have been openly expressed—sometimes with hostility. In these communities there is no advantage or special recognition bestowed on expressions of ethnicity. They recognize that their congregations have been configured in a particular way by Mexican culture ("...Mexicans are like, *devoted*"). The valuing of their ethnic heritage through an ethnic church takes place in the absence of any ethos of multiculturalism, in other words their expressions of ethnic solidarity are *less* a conscious strategy of assertion than a natural orbit around the familial and cultural gravity of "my people."

While these three congregations represent different religious traditions, they nevertheless have similar effects on the mobility and acculturation paths of these youth.

Both kinds of communities promoted education and a work ethnic, and had practical and material payoffs. The Protestant groups did reject some traditional elements of collective religious expression, but for spiritual rather than assimilationist reasons. They continued to act as agents of ethnic socialization, functioning to reinforce cultural values (that met "Biblical" criteria) and continued to provide a bridge to the ethnic community.

Compared to what Herberg and Hansen found earlier in the century, the Latino second generation represents evidence of a fundamental departure in how it finds its identity within a religio-ethnic community. It is not in the "absence of immigrant foreignness" that they have found their place in American society, but in communities that remember and reenact their *foreign* roots. While religious identity would not disappear in the absence of an ethnic community of faith, for these youth that is where it finds its *most natural* expression. These youth have not jettisoned the cultural baggage of the ethnic faith community to better their chances for upward mobility.

The presence of the Latino second generation in these congregations, however, also presents a challenge to the communities of memory. Rather than being simply on the receiving end of measures to control them, the second generation youth are actors in a process of creating new forms of cultural and religious expression. To describe these congregations as "reservoirs of culture" is likewise inadequate, for it suggests that they are cultural backwaters that primarily serve a marginalized first generation who live in the past. But congregations where the second generation have a stake in the future become the "locus" of new cultural identities. A critical mass of second-generation youth pushes the community of memory to also become a community of change.

RESEARCH DIRECTIONS

During the course of this study I have identified a number of questions that merit further inquiry.

The Long View

A longitudinal study which tracked the actual participation of the second generation would be useful in learning more about the *calculus of choice* for continued involvement. There is nothing in their current narratives to suggest that they are just waiting for the right time to make their escape, when they must no longer be there "out of respect" for parents. Most say they plan to raise their own families in these faith communities. Will these attitudes stand the test of time? To what extent will it hinge on their own desires and aspirations for their children, and on the sensibilities of their marital partners.

Family Metaphors

Chinese Protestant and Latino congregations have both been able to attract a significant number of the second generation. Both of them are similar in that they emphasize the congregation as a "family" and as a place where family values are affirmed, and reconciliation of relationships can take place. It appears that family issues matter greatly to the second generation. The question arises about how the Latino experience compares with other second generation youth in their decision to stay in the ethnic church.

Latinos and Race

The question of race within Latino congregations is an interesting one. Their religious congregations, while united around core cultural values, often racially mixed. Where racial differences are frequently the dividing line between Caucasian and Black congregations, they are not for Latinos. Latino congregations may be redefining the meaning of race within religious communities.

Class and Social Capital

Religion has been identified as an increasingly vital source of social capital (Stevens-Arroyo 2000). For groups such as the Vietnamese of Bankston and Zhou's study, who reside in a low-income ghettos, upward mobility hinges upon integration into the ethnic community with its attendant social capital. However, if groups settle in middle class white environments (as do many Asian Indians), they don't rely on co-ethnic social capital for advancement as much, since middle-class society provides it. In the study at hand, Latinos are settling into communities that are either semi-rural working class, or middle-class rural communities. These communities have decent educational and health infrastructure (in part due to the efforts of professional class Latinos). Demand for the labor of the Latino working poor and working class is high, and very few Latino adults are unemployed. To what extent then do Latino youth rely on sources of social capital within the ethnic congregation?

Epilogue

It is now late June; Monday's paper has a front-page article about a family at St. Barbara's whose two children will be going to the University of Michigan. Throughout the summer Danny drives a forklift at a packinghouse; he works overtime during cherry and apple season. Cristiana is working as a teacher's aid at the middle school. In the fall she will be a starter for the Ciderville Indian's Basketball team. In Meyerton, Almira's picture appears in the local paper along with a short article she wrote about her sometimes-painful experiences as a Latina at Meyerton High. Estela is still at *PJs Burritos*, waiting tables for a mostly Amish clientele. She'll be a freshman in the fall, taking communications and living at a university 50 miles away, but commuting back home on the weekends.

For Arturo Jr. and his family, their journey is not over. The economic boom and the relocation of plants to non-unionized areas such as Meyerton continue to attract Mexican families. Both his and his uncle's family have moved to Meyerton where better paying industrial jobs are more plentiful. By coincidence he and his cousin Ruth will go to Meyerton High and most likely sit in classes with the students from Templo Rey who participated in my focus group. Ruth will no doubt spend some time in Megan's ESL class.

As so many other field workers have done, I venture out on the thin ice of personal involvement. After discovering that they had moved, I called some of the Templo Rey youth to give them a heads up, to look out for Arturo and Ruth, try to lend a helping hand and be a friend. I contact Megan to look out for "my friends." I even suggest their name to a potential employer. (So much for detachment.) Fortunately I will not lose contact with them that easily. Even though *Templo Rey* is five minutes from their door, they say they plan to continue driving each Saturday two hours each way to *Iglesia Adventista* at Berryville (15 minutes from my house).

Javier, from *Templo*, will start college in the fall. Over fries at McDonalds he tells me why he stopped attending for a year; he felt that the youth pastor neglected the American born youth. He tells me about his recent conversion experience, precipitated by a brush with the law, and his tremendous respect for his father. He feels God has called him back to *Templo* for a particular mission—to reach out to those like himself—"I'm a mix, a Chicano" he says. "We are attempting to create something else..."

Notes

[1] The Latinos population is much more ethnically diverse than this sample. While most Latinos in the Midwest are of Mexican descent, there are growing numbers from Central America, the Caribbean, and South America are also present (see Millard and Chapa, forthcoming).
[2] Quoting an observation made by Marie Marquart during the Annual Meeting of the American Sociological Society, August 11, 2000.

Appendices

Appendix 1: Profile of Interview Respondents
(N = 50)

Ethnicity	Mexican=30 Puerto Rican=1 Columbian=1 Anglo=18
Sex	Female=27 Male=33
Country of Birth	US=42 Mexico=6 Puerto Rico=1 Columbia=1
Occupation	HS Student=19 College student=2 Clergy=8 Education=10 City/state gov=5 Self-employed=2 Journalist=2 Retired=2
Age	<20 yrs =18 20-30 =9 30-40=3 40-50=8 >50=12

Appendix 2: In-depth Interview Schedule

(Note--in the first interview I introduce myself, explain more about project, make sure youth and parents are given consent form, ask some general ice breaker questions about school, work, sports etc.)

1. Life history:
Tell me some things about you and your family--where your parents are from, where you were born, where you've lived, where you've gone to school. In thinking about your experience, has it been good? Has it been tough in some ways? (The life history question, like the others, can be continued in subsequent interviews).

2. Social adjustment:
Tell me more about school. What subjects do you like best? How are your grades? Do you have a lot of friends at school? Do you like the teachers?
Tell me more about your job. How many hours do you work each week? What do you like about it? Do you get along well with your co-workers, your boss? What are the greatest difficulties that you presently experience?

3. Social network:
Tell me who are the most important people in your life? Why are they important? Who are your best friends? What language do you speak with these people? Do you keep in close contact with relative and friends in Mexico?

4. Religious participation and identity:

Tell me about your church.   Did you always attend a Latino church? Why do you prefer Latino churches over English speaking churches? Do you study the bible and your lesson in Spanish? How often do you attend Sunday School, catechism, Divine service, *culto*, youth meetings (*sociedad de jovenes*) prayer meetings? If someone were to ask you, "what religion are you?" how would you answer them? Do you want to work for the church some day?

5. Identity:

a) When you think about describing yourself to other people, what are the three most important ways in defining who you are?, (for example as a Christian, a Catholic, the son or daughter of "so and so", as a Dominican, etc.) Another way to ask this is to ask them to fill in the blank to the question: "I am _____. "

6. Ethnic identity:

How do you identify yourself with respect to your parent's culture? Do you consider yourself Hispanic, Latino, Mexican, Chicano, Dominican-American etc.? Do you feel that by growing up in two worlds, that of your parents, and that of American culture, has given you a unique experience and identity? Could you say that you feel completely "American"? Are you embarrassed by when your parents speak Spanish in public? Do you feel accepted by people outside of your ethic group? What language did you speak at work? At home? With friends? At church? Do you consider yourself fluent in English?

7. <u>Relationship with parents:</u>
How would you describe your relationship with your parents? Do you feel like they understand how it is to grow up in this country? Do your parents criticize you for being too American? Are your parents able to help you with homework?

8. <u>Involvement in ethnic organizations:</u>
Outside of church, do you meet with any organized group of (Mexican, Latino) people? Do you frequent music stores, food stores, restaurants, clubs, where Spanish is spoken or products from Latin America are sold?

9. <u>The future</u>:
What plans do you have after graduating from high school (or college)? What are your career goals? Do you want to attend college? What do you imagine yourself doing in 10 years?

10. Any other questions that arise out of interview.

References

Abalos, David. 1986. *Latinos in the United States.* South Bend, IN: University of Notre Dame Press.

Abramson, Harold J. 1980. "Religion," Pp. 869-875 in *Harvard Encyclopedia of American Ethnic Groups*, edited by Stephan Thernstrom. Cambridge, MA: Belknap.

Alba, Richard, and Nee, Victor. 1996. "The Assimilation of Immigrant Groups: Concept, Theory and Evidence. " Presented at the Conference on "Becoming American/America Becoming: International Migration to the United States," January 18-21, sponsored by the Social Science Research Council.

Ainsley, Ricardo. 1998. "Cultural Mourning, Immigration, and Engagement: Vignettes from the Mexican Experience." Pp. 283 – 300, in *Crossings: Mexican Immigration in Interdisciplinary Perspectives.* Edited by M. Suarez-Orozco. Cambridge, MA: Harvard University/David Rockefellar Center for Latin American Studies.

Ainsworth-Darnell and Downey, Victor. 1998. "Assessing the Oppositional Culture Explanation for Racial/Ethnic Differences in School Performance." *American Sociological Review*, 63: 536-553.

Allensworth, Elaine and Refugio I. Rochin. 1999. *The Mexicanization of Rural California.* Michigan State University. Julian Samora Research Institute.

Alstott, Owen, (ed). 1989. *Flor y canto.* Portland, OR: Oregon Catholic Press.

Anderson, Robert Mapes. 1979. *Vision of the Disinherited*. New York: Oxford University Press.

Aponte, Robert. 1997. "Winds of Change Sweep Nation as Latino Population Grows." *NEXO*, Vol V, No. 2.

Aponte, Robert and Marcelo Siles. 1995. "The Browning of the Midwest." *NEXO*, vol. IV. 1995 no. 1.

Armendariz, Rubén, P. 1999. "The Protestant Hispanic Congregation: Identity." Pp. 239-254 in *Protestantes/Protestants: Hispanic Christianity within Mainline Traditions*, edited by D. Maldonado Jr. Nashville: Abingdon.

Bankston, Carl I., III, and Min Zhou. 1998. "Growing Up American." New York: Russell Sage Foundation.

_____. 1996. "The Ethnic Church, Ethnic Identification, and the Social Adjustment of Vietnamese Adolescents." *Review of Religious Research*, 38, No. 1. pp. 18-37.

Becker, Penny. 1999. *Congregations in Conflict: Cultural Models of Local Religious Life*. Cambridge: Cambridge University Press.

Bellah, Robert, N., et. al. 1996. *Habits of the Heart*. Berkeley, CA: University of California Press.

Berger, Peter. 1967. *The Sacred Canopy: Elements of a Sociological Theory of Religion*. Garden City: Anchor Books.

Brittain, Carmina, 2002. Transnational Messages: Experiences of Chinese and Mexican Immigrants in American Schools. New York: LFB Scholarly Publishing.

Buroway, Michael et. al. 1991. "The Extended Case Method." Pp. 271-287in *Ethnography Unbound: Power and Resistance in the Modern Metropolis*. Berkeley: University of California Press.

Cerulo, Karen. 1997. "Identity Construction." Pp. 385-402 in *Annual Review of Sociology* , edited by John Hagan and Karen Cook, Vol. 23.

Chai, Karen J. 1998. "Competing for the Second Generation: English-Language Ministry at a Korean Protestant Church." Pp. 265-294, in *Gatherings in Diaspora: Religious Communities and the New Immigration* , edited by R. S. Warner and K. Wittner. Philadelphia: Temple University Press.

Chapa, Jorge, Richard R. Valencia. 1993. "Latino Population Growth, Demographic Characteristics, and Education Stagnation: An Examination of Recent Trends." *Hispanic Journal of Behavioral Sciences,* 15:2.

Chavez, Leo. 1998. *Shadowed Lives: Undocumented Immigrants in American Society.* San Diego, CA: Wadsworth.

Commission on Immigration Reform. 1997. *Binational Study: Migration Between Mexico and the United States: A Report of the Binational Study on Migration.*

Cox, Harvey. *Fire From Heaven.* 1995. Reading MA: Addison Wesley.

Crane, Ken. 1997. "The Role of the Ethnic Church in Selective Acculturation: A Comparative Ethnography of Hispanic and Korean Youth." Unpublished manuscript.

Crane, Ken 1998. "Religious Adaptation of Latino/a Adventist Youth: Findings from AVANCE". *Latino Studies Journal,* 9:2, pp. 74-103.

Davidman, Lynn. 1991. *Tradition in a Rootless World: Women Turn to Orthodox Judaism.* Berkeley, CA: University of California Press.

Deck, Allan F. 1994. "The Challenge of Evangelical/Pentecostal
    Christianity to Hispanic Catholicism." Pp. 409-439, in
    Hispanic Catholic Culture in the U.S . edited by J. Dolan
    and F. Deck. Notre Dame, IN: Notre Dame University
    Press.

Diaz-Stevens, Ana Maria. 1993. *Oxcart Catholicism on Fifth
    Avenue*. Notre Dame, IN: Notre Dame University Press.

Dolan, Jay P. 1983. *The Immigrant Church*. Notre Dame, IN:
    University of Notre Dame Press.

Dorsey, Patricia. 2000. "Whomsoever Will: Southwest Assembly of
    God. Pp. 291-324, in *Religion and the New Immigrants:
    Continuities And Adaptations In Immigrant Congregations*,
    edited by H. Ebaugh and J. Chafetz. Walnut Creek, CA:
    AltaMira Press.

Durkheim, Emile. 1947.*The Division of Labor in Society* . New
    York: Free Press.

Ebaugh, Helen R. and Janet S. Chavetz. 2000. *Religion and the New
    Immigrants: Continuities And Adaptations In Immigrant
    Congregations*. Walnut Creek, CA: AltaMira Press.

Ebaugh, Helen R. and Janet S. Chavetz, eds. Forthcoming. *Religion
    Across Borders: Transnational Immigrant Networks*. Walnut
    Creek, CA: AltaMira Press.

Erikson, Erik H. 1959. *Identity and the Life Cycle*. New York:
    International Universities Press.

Elizondo, Virgilio P. 1988. *The Future is Mestizo*. Bloomington, IN:
    Meyer-Stone.

_____. 1990. *forward, Manana: Christian Theology from a Latino
    Perspective*. Nashville, TN: Abingdon.

Fenton, John Y. 1988. *Transplanting Religious Traditions: Asian Indians in America.* New York: Praeger.

Fernández Kelly, and Richard Schauffler. 1996. "Divided Fates: Immigrant Children and the New Assimilation." Pp. 30-53, in *The New Second Generation*, edited by A. Portes. New York: Russell Sage Foundation.

Finke, Roger, and Laurence R. Iannaccone. 1993. "Supply Side Explanations for Religious Change." *The Annals of the American Academy of Political and Social Science.* 527: 27-39.

Fix, Michael and Passel, Jeffrey S. 1994. *Immigration and Immigrants: Setting the Record Straight.* Washington D.C.: The Urban Institute.

Fishkin, Barbara. 1997. *Muddy Cup.* New York: Scribner.

Gans, Herbert. 1979. "Symbolic Ethnicity: The Future of Ethnic Groups and Cultures in America, " *Ethnic and Racial Studies*, 2: 1-20.

_____. 1992. "Second Generation Decline: Scenario for the Economic and Ethnic Futures of the Post-1965 American Immigrants," *Ethnic and Racial Studies*, 15, 2: 173-192.

Geertz, Clifford. 1966. "Religion as a Cultural System." Pp. 1-46, in *Anthropological Approaches to the Study of Religion*, edited by M. Banton. London: Tavistock.

_____. 1973. *The Interpretation of Cultures.* New York: Basic Books.

George, Sheba. 1998. "Caroling with the Keralites" Pp. 265-294, in *Gatherings in Diaspora: Religious Communities and the New Immigration*, edited by R. S. Warner and E. Wittner. Philadelphia: Temple University Press.

Gibson, Margaret. 1995. "Additive Acculturation as a Strategy for
     School Improvement." Pp. 77-106, in *California's
     Immigrant Children: Theory, Research, and Implications
     for Educational Policy* , edited by R. G. Rumbaut and W.
     Cornelius. San Diego, CA: Center for U.S. Mexican
     Studies.

Glazer, N. 1993. "Is Assimilation Dead?" *The Annals of the
     American Academy of Political and Social Science*, 530:
     122-136.

Gleason, P. 1981. "American Identity and Americanization." Pp.
     31-58 in *Harvard Encyclopedia of American Ethnic
     Groups.*, edited by S. Thernstrom. Cambridge, MA:
     Harvard University Press.

Goette, Robert. 1993. "Transformation of First Generation Church into
     a Bilingual Second Generation Church." Pp. 237-252 in *The
     Emerging Generations of Korean-Americans* , edited by H.
     Kwon and S. Kim. Soeul: Kyung Hee University Press.

Goizueta, Roberto S. 1995. *Caminemos con Jesús: Toward a
     Hispanic/Latino Theology of Accompaniment*. Maryknoll,
     NY: Orbis Press.

Gold, Stephan J. 1989. "Differential Adjustment Among New
     Immigrant Family Members." *Journal of Contemporary
     Ethnography* , 17:4.

_____. 1992. *Refugee Communities: A Comparative Field Study*.
     Thousand Oaks, CA: Sage.

_____. 1995. *From the Workers' State to the Golden State: Jews
     from the Former Soviet Union in California*. Needham
     Heights, MA: Allyn and Bacon.

_____. 1998. "What is Ethnicity?" Unpublished manuscript.

Gordon, Milton M. 1964. *Assimilation in American Life*. New York: Oxford University Press.

Greeley, Andrew M. 1972. *The Denominational Society*. Glenview, IL: Scott, Foresman.

_____. 1988. "Defection Among Latinos." *America*, July, pp. 61-62

Griffith, David and Ed Kassam. 1997. *Working Poor: Farmworkers in the U.S.* Philadelphia: Temple University Press.

Groody, Daniel G., 2002. Border of Death, Valley of Life. Walnut Creek, CA: AltaMira Press.

Gutiérrez, David G. 1998. "Ethnic Mexicans and the Transformation of American Public Space: Reflections on Recent History." Pp. 307 – 340, in *Crossings: Mexican Immigration in Interdisciplinary Perspectives*, edited by M. Suarez-Orozco. Cambridge, MA: Harvard University/David Rockefellar Center for Latin American Studies.

Hallum, Anne Motley. 1996. *Beyond Missionaries: Toward an Understanding of the Protestant Movement in Central America*. New York: Rowan & Littlefield.

Hammond, Philip E. 1988. "Religion and the Persistence of Identity." *Journal for the Scientific Study of Religion*, 27: 1-11.

Hammond, Phillip and Warner, Kee. 1993. "Religion and Ethnicity in Late-Twentieth Century America." *The Annals of the American Academy of Political and Social Science,*, 527: 55-66.

Handlin, Oscar. 1951. *The Uprooted: The Epic Story of the Great Migrations That Made the American People*. Boston: Little, Brown.

Hansen, Marcus Lee. 1940. *The Problem of the Third Generation Immigrant*. Rock Island, IL: Augustana Historical Society.

Heo, J. 1998. *Between Two Worlds.* (Videotape), Berkeley, CA:
    Center for Media and Independant Learning.

Herberg, Will. 1955. *Protestant--Catholic--Jew: An essay in
    American Religious Sociology.* New York: Doubleday.

Hernández, Edwin I. 1995. "The Browning of Adventism." *Spectrum,*
    December, pp. 25-50.

_____. 1999. "Moving from the Cathedral to Store Front Churches:
    Understanding Religious Growth and Decline among Latino
    Protestants." Pp. 216-238 in *Protestantes/Protestants:
    Hispanic Christianity within Mainline Traditions,* edited by D.
    Maldonado Jr. Nashville: Abingdon.

_____. 1999a. "Moving from the Cathedral to Store Front Churches:
    Understanding Religious Growth and Decline among Latino
    Protestants." Lilly Project. Unpublished Manuscript.

Hernández, Edwin I. and Roger Dudley. 1990. "Persistence of Religion
    Through Primary Group Ties Among Latino Seventh-day
    Adventist Young People." *Review of Religious Research.* 32:
    157-172.

Hirschman, Charles, et. al. *The Handbook of International Migration.*
    1999. New York: Russel Sage Foundation.

Hondogneu-Sotelo, Pierette. 1994. *Gendered Transitions: Mexican
    Experiences of Immigration.* Berkeley, CA: University of
    California Press.

Huddle, Donald. 1994. "The Net National Costs of Immigration in
    1993." Washington D.C.: Carrying Capacity Network.

Hurh, Won Moo and Kwang Chung Kim. 1984. *Korean Immigrants in
    America: A Structural Analysis of Ethnic Confinement and
    Adhesive Adaptation.* Madison, N.J.: Fairleigh Dickinson
    University Press.

_____. 1990. "Religious Participation of Korean Immigrants in the United States." *Journal for the Scientific Study of Religion* 29: 19-34.

Huynh, Thuan. 2000. "Center for Vietnamese Buddhism: Recreating Home." Pp. 45-66 in *Religion and the New Immigrants: Continuities and Adaptations in Immigrant Congregations*, edited by Helen R. Ebaugh and Janet S. Chavetz. Walnut Creek, CA: AltaMira Press.

Iannaccone, Laurence R. 1994. "Why Strict Churches are Strong." *American Journal of Sociology*. 99: 1180-1211.

Jacobson, Jessica. 1997. "Religion and Ethnicity: Dual and Alternative Sources of Identity Among Young British Pakistanis." *Ethnic and Racial Studies*, 20: 238-56.

Jefferds, Maria. 1999. "Increasing Latino Settlement in Two Towns in Rural Michigan: Community and Institutional Responses." Department of Anthropology, Michigan State University. Unpublished manuscript.

Jensen, Leif and Yoshimi Chitose 1996. Today's Second Generation: Evidence from the 1990 Census." Pp 82-107 in *The New Second Generation* , edited by A. Portes. New York: Russell Sage.

Kashima, Tetsuden. 1990. "The Buddhist Chuches of America: Challenges for Change in the 21st Century." *Pacific World*. 6: 28-40.

Keysar, Ariela, Barry A. Kosmin and Egon Mayer. 2002. *Religious Identification Among Hispanics in the United States*. Office of Research for Religion in Society and Culture, Brooklyn College of CUNY, Brooklyn, New York.

Kibria, Nazli. 1994. *Family Tightrope: The Changing Lives of Vietnamese Americans*. Princeton: Princeton University Press.

Kim, David Kyuman. 1993. "Becoming: Korean Americans, Faith, and Identity--Observations on an Emerging Culture." Master of Divinity thesis, Harvard Divinity School.

Kim, Illsoo. 1981. *New Urban Immigrants: The Korean Community in New York.* Princeton: Princeton University Press.

Kurien, Prema. 1998. "Becoming American by Becoming Hindu: Indian Americans Take Their Place at the Multicultural Table." Pp. 37-70 in *Gatherings in Diaspora: Religious Communities and the New Immigration*, edited by R. S. Warner and E. Wittner. Philadelphia: Temple University Press.

Kwon, Okyun. 2003. Buddhist and Protestant Korean Immigrants.

Lamont, Michèle and Marcel Fournier. 1992. "Introduction" in *Cultivating Differences: Symbolic Boundaries and the Making of Inequality*, edited by M. Lamont and M. Fournier: Chicago: University of Chicago Press.

Lawson, Ronald. 1999. "When Immigrants Take Over: The Impact of Immigrant Growth on American Seventh-day Adventism's Trajectory from Sect to Denomination." *Journal for the Scientific Study of Religion*, 38 (1): 83-102.

León, Luís D. 1998. "Born Again in East Los Angeles: The Congregation as Border Space." Pp. 163-196 in *Gatherings in Diaspora: Religious Communities and the New Immigration*, edited by R. S. Warner and E. Wittner. Philadelphia: Temple University Press.

Leonard, Karen Isaksen. 1992. *Making Ethnic Choices: California's Punjabi Mexican Americans.* Philadelphia: Temple University Press.

Lewis, William F. 1993. *Soul Rebels: The Rastafari.* Prospect Heights, IL: Waveland Press.

Lincoln, Yvonna S. and Egon G. Guba. 1985. "Postpositivism and the Naturalist Paradigm." Pp. 14-46 in *Naturalistic Inquiry*, Newbury Park, CA: Sage.

Maldonado, David. Jr., ed. 1999. *Protestantes/Protestants: Hispanic Christianity within Mainline Traditions,.* Nashville: Abingdon.

Marín, Gerardo, and Barbara VanOss Marín. 1991. *Research With Hispanic Populations.* Newberry Park, CA: Sage.

Martin, Phillip, J. Edward Taylor and Michael Fix. "Immigration and the Changing Face of Rural America: Focus on the Midwestern States." JSRI Occasional Paper #21, The Julian Samora Research Institute. Michigan State University, East Lansing, Michigan.

Massey, Douglas S. and Nancy A. Denton. 1985. "Spatial Assimilation as a Socioeconomic Outcome."*American Sociological Review* 50: 94-106.

Massey, et.al. "An Evaluation of International Migration Theory: The North American Case." *Population Development Review*, 20, 4: 699-752.

Massey, Douglas. 1995. "The New Immigration and Ethnicity in the United States." *Population and Development Review*, 21, 3: 631-652.

MacLeod, Jay. 1995. *Ain't No Makin' It*. Boulder, CO: Westview.

Matute-Bianchi, M.E. 1986. "Ethnic Identities and Patterns of School Success and Failure Among Mexican-descent and Japanese-American Students in a California High School: An Ethnographic Analysis." *American Journal of Education*, 95, 233-255.

Millard, Ann V. 1998. Keynote Address for Southwest Michigan Migrant Resource Council, Lawrence, Michigan.

Millard Ann V., and Jorge Chapa. Forthcoming. *Apple Pie and Enchiladas: Latino Newcomers and the Changing Dynamics of the Rural Midwest.* Austin, TX: University of Texas Press.

Min, Pyong Gap. 1992. "The Structure and Social Functions of Korean Immigrant Churches in the United States." *International Migration Review* 26, 4: 1370-1394.

Mittleberg, David, and Mary C. Waters. 1992. "The Process of Ethnogenesis Among Haitian and Israeli Immigrants in the United States." *Ethnic and Racial Studies* 15: 412-435.

Moore, Joan and Raquel Pinderhughes, eds. 1993. *In the Barrios: Latinos and the Underclass Debate.* New York: Russell Sage Foundation.

Murdoch, George P. 1987. *Outline of Cultural Materials*, 5th ed. New Haven, CN: Human Relations Area Files, Inc.

Neitz, Mary Jo. 1990. "Studying Religion in the Eighties." Pp. 90-118 *in Symbolic Interaction and Cultural Studies*, edited by Howard Becker and Michael McCall. Chicago: University of Chicago Press.

Niebuhr, Gustav. 1999. "Across America, Immigration Is Changing the Face of Religion." New York Times, September 23.

Niebuhr, H. Richard. 1929. *The Social Sources of Denominationalism.* New York: Henry Holt.

Ogbu, J.U. 1991. "Immigrant and Involuntary Minorities in Comparative Perspective." Pp. 3-33 in *Minority Status and Schooling: A Comparative Study of Immigrant and Involuntary Minorities* , edited by M.A. Gibson and J.U. Obgu. New York: Garland Press.

Oropesa, R. S., and Nancy S. Landale. 1997. "In Search of the New Second Generation." *Sociological Perspectives.* 40: 3: 426-455.

Pedraza, Sylvia, and Rubén G. Rumbaut. 1996. *Origins and Destinies: Immigration, Race, and Ethnicity in America.*

Peréz, Jason. 2003. "Community Study of Sunset Park, New York." Presented at the PARAL Study Convocation, January 9, San Germán, Puerto Rico.

Ponciano, Maria. 2003. "Community Study of Union City." Presented at the PARAL Study Convocation, January 9, San Germán, Puerto Rico.

Portes, Alejandro. 1995. "Children of immigrants: Segmented Assimilation and its Determinants." Pp. 248-27 in *The Economic Sociology of Immigration: Essays on Networks, Ethnicity, and Entrepreneurship*, edited by A. Portes. New York: Russell Sage Foundation.

_____, ed. 1996. *The New Second Generation.* New York: Russell Sage.

Portes, Alejandro, and Rubén G. Rumbaut. 1996. 2nd ed. *Immigrant America: A Portrait.* Berkeley. CA: University of California Press.

Portes, Alejandro and Rubén G. Rumbaut. 2001. *Legacies: The Story of the New Second Generation.* Berkeley. CA: University of California Press.

Portes, Alejandro, and Julia Sessenbrenner. 1993. "Embeddedness and Immigration: Notes on the Social Determinants of Economic Action." *American Journal of Sociology* 98: 1320-1350.

Rochin, Refugio I. and Marcelo E. Siles. 1994. "Michigan's
    Farmworkers: A Status Report on Employment and Housing."
    Statistical Brief No. 2, Julian Samora Research Institute.
    Michigan State University, East Lansing, Michigan.

Rodriguez, Richard. 1992. *Days of Obligation: An Argument with my
    Mexican Father*. New York: Penguin.

Roof, Wade Clark. 1993. "Toward the Year 2000:
    Reconstructions of Religious Space." *The Annals of the
    American Academy of Political and Social Science*. 527:
    155-170.

Rosenbaum, Rene. 1996. "Growth of Latinos in Michigan." *NEXO*,
    Fall, Vol. V, No. 1. The Julian Samora Research Institute.
    Michigan State University, East Lansing, Michigan.

Rothenberg, Daniel. 1998. *With These Hands: The Hidden World of
    Migrant Farmworkers Today*. New York: Harcourt Brace.

Rumbaut, Rubén. G. 1994. "The Crucible Within: Ethnic Identity,
    Self-Esteem, and Segmented Assimilation Among
    Children of Immigrants." *International Migration Review*,
    28: 748-794.

_____. 1997. "Paradoxes (and Orthodoxes) of Assimilation."
    Sociological Forces.

_____. 1999. "Assimilation and its Discontents: Ironies and
    Paradoxes. 172-195 in *International Handbook of
    Migration*., edited by C. Hirschman, et. al. New York:
    Russel Sage Foundation.

Rumbaut, Rubén, G. and Wayne A. Cornelius,. eds. *California's
    Immigrant Children: Theory, Research, and Implications
    for Educational Policy*. San Diego, CA: Center for U.S. -
    Mexican Studies.

Rutledge, Paul James. 1992. *The Vietnamese Experience in America.* Bloomington: Indiana University Press.

Saenz, Rogelio, and Cynthia M. Cready. 1996. "The Southwest-Midwest Mexican American Migration Flows, 1985-1990." Paper presented at the 1996 Annual Meeting of the Rural Sociological Society, Des Moines, Iowa.

Sandburg, Carl. 1960. *Harvest Poems 1910-1960.* New York: Harcourt Brace Jovanovich.

Sandell, David. 2003. "The Daily Service, An Introduction." Presented at the PARAL Study Convocation, January 10, San Germán, Puerto Rico.

Sengupta, Somini. 1999. "On One Queens Block, Many Prayers Are Spoken." New York Times, November 7.

Smith, Timothy. 1978. "Religion and Ethnicity in America." *American Historical Review* 83 (December): 1155-1185.

Stark, Rodney and William S. Bainbridge. 1985. *The Future of Religion: Secularization, Revival, and Cult Formation.* Berkeley: University of California Press.

Stark, Rodney and Laurence R. Iannaccone,. 1993. "Rational Choice Propositions about Religious Movements," *Religion and the Social Order* 3: 241-261.

Stevens-Arroyo, Anthony M., Anneris Goris and Ariela Keysar. 2002. *The PARAL Study: The National Survey of Leadership in Latino Parishes and Congregations.* Office of Research for Religion in Society and Culture, Brooklyn College of CUNY, Brooklyn, New York.

Stoll, David. 1990. *Is Latin America Turning Protestant? The Politics of Evangelical Growth.* Berkeley: University of California Press.

Strauss, Anselm. L. 1987. *Qualitative Analysis for Social Scientists.*
    Cambridge: Cambridge University Press.

Suarez-Orozco, Marcelo, ed. 1998. *Crossings, Mexican Immigration
    in Interdisciplinary Perspectives.* Cambridge MA: Center for
    Latin American Studies and Harvard University Press.

Sullivan, Kathleen. 2000. "Iglesia de Dios: An Extended Family." Pp.
    141-152 in *Religion and the New Immigrants: Continuities
    And Adaptations In Immigrant Congregations.* edited by H.
    Ebaugh and J. Chafetz. Walnut Creek, CA: AltaMira Press.

Swidler, Ann. 1986 "Culture in Action: Symbols and Strategies,"
    American Sociological Review 51 (April): 273-286.

Valdes, D. 1990. *Al Norte: Agricultural Workers in the Great Lakes
    Region, 1917-1970.* Austin: UT Press.

Viadero, Debra. 2000. "Generation Gap."*Education Week* , June 7, pp.
    28-30.

Warner, Stephan. 1993. "Work in Progress toward a New
    Paradigm for the Sociological Study of Religion in the
    United States."*American Journal of Sociology* 98:1044-
    93.

_____. 1996. "Perspectives on New Ethnic and Immigrant
    Congregations." Chicago: NIECP, University of Illinois at
    Chicago, Office of Social Research.

Warner, Stephan, and E. Wittner, eds. 1998. *Gatherings in
    Diaspora: Religious Communities and the New
    Immigration,* Philadelphia: Temple University Press.

Weber, M. 1948. "The Protestant Sects and the Spirit of Capitalism."
    Pp. 302-322, in *Max Weber: Essays in Sociology*, edited by H.
    Gerth and C.W. Mills. London: K.Paul, Tench, Trubner.

Weber M. 1930. *The Protestant Ethic and the Spirit of Capitalism..* Translated by Talcott Parsons. London: George Allen & Unwin LTD.

Williams, Raymond B. 1988. *Religions of Immigrants from India and Pakistan: New Threads in the American Tapestry.* Cambridge University Press.

Willis, Paul. 1977. *Learning to Labor.* Aldershot: Gower.

Wilson, Bryan. 1982. *Religion in Sociological Perspective.* New York: Oxford University Press.

Woldemikael, Tekle M. 1987. "Assertion Versus Acommodation: A Comparative Approach to Intergroup Relations." *American Behavioral Scientist* 30, 4: 411-428.

Yang, Fenggang. 1999. *Chinese Christians in America.* University Park, PA: Pennsylvania State University Press.

_____. 2000. "Chinese Gospel Church: The Sinicization of Christianity." Pp. 89-108 in *Religion and the New Immigrants: Continuities And Adaptations In Immigrant Congregations,* edited by H. Ebaugh and J. S. Chavetz. Walnut Creek, CA: AltaMira Press.

Zhou, Min. 1999. "Segmented Assimilation: Issues, Controversies, and Recent Research on the New Second Generation." Pp. 196-211 in *Handbook of International Migration, edited by* C. Hirschman, et. al. New York: Russel Sage Foundation.

Index

Printed in the United States
89826LV00001B/55-66/A